WOMEN'S ECONOMIC EMPOWERMENT IN THE PACIFIC REGION

A COMPREHENSIVE ANALYSIS OF EXISTING RESEARCH AND DATA

MAY 2023

ASIAN DEVELOPMENT BANK

ADB

Notes:
In this publication, "$" refers to United States dollars, unless otherwise stated.
ADB recognizes "China" as the People's Republic of China, "East Timor" as Timor-Leste, "Republic of Marshall Islands" as the Republic of the Marshall Islands, and "Vietnam" as Viet Nam.

Cover design by Edith Creus.

On the cover, *main photo:* Dancers at a cultural presentation in Rarotonga, the Cook Islands. *Other photos from left to right:* Wives of the workers at the Guadalcanal Plains Palm Oil company taking part in a sewing course initiative in the outskirts of Honiara, Solomon Islands; Christine Memti, driver of IPI Transport and beneficiary of the Kotna-Lampramp road subproject, PNG; and Women delivering fruits in Rakiraki, Nadi (Photos by ADB).

Photo credit: All photos are ADB.

Contents

Tables, Figures, and Boxes

Foreword

Women's economic empowerment is vital to realizing women's rights, reducing poverty, and achieving gender equality across the globe. When more women undertake paid work, economies expand through enhanced productivity, economic diversification, and income equality. If women's earnings increase and become more stable, other areas of women's lives also improve. They can afford health care, can pay for their children's school fees, and are more likely to play a leadership role in their communities. Women's economic empowerment is therefore a win-win situation that can help not only women but also the community and society.

Despite the clear business case for investing in women's work, too often women end up in insecure, low-wage, and low-skilled jobs that have exploitative and unequal working conditions, and they are often in the informal economy. As women perform the bulk of unpaid care work, they often have little time for paid work. This situation also exists in the Pacific where barriers to women's economic participation, progression, voice, and agency stubbornly persist despite economic growth, decreasing fertility rates, and increased access to education. Evidence shows that women have been disproportionately affected by the economic fallout from the coronavirus disease (COVID-19) pandemic.

The Asian Development Bank (ADB) recognizes that to reduce poverty rates, helping women and girls must be a priority in its work. Women's economic empowerment is essential for meeting the Pacific's aspirations of inclusive and sustainable development. As part of its Strategy 2030, ADB aims to help create decent work opportunities for women, especially in higher value-added entrepreneurship. This reflects ADB's support for its developing member countries in making progress toward the Sustainable Development Goals, particularly Goal 5 to achieve gender equality, and Goal 8, to promote full and productive employment and decent work for all.

This report helps establish the evidence base for ADB Pacific developing member countries as they determine what research gaps to fill, which social norms to disrupt, and which policies to reform. We hope that this report will catalyze discussion and action among ADB, Pacific governments, women's civil society groups, and the private sector, with the aim of building a more inclusive economy for all.

Leah Gutierrez
Director General
Pacific Department
Asian Development Bank

Acknowledgments

This literature review was prepared by Social Development Direct: Chris Hearle (team leader), Olivia Jenkins, and Rebekah Martin, with quality assurance by Gillian Brown, Erika Fraser, and Isabelle Cardinal. The report significantly benefited from inputs and reviews by staff and consultants at the Asian Development Bank including Emily Brearley, Cindy Bryson, Mairi Macrae, and Keiko Nowacka. Peer reviewers included Sarah Boxall, Ingrid FitzGerald, Malika Shagazatova, and Sabine Spohn. Cecilia Caparas (knowledge management officer) managed the publication production process. Cyrel San Gabriel copyedited the publication and Edith Creus provided design and layout services. This literature review has been funded by the Women Entrepreneurs Funding Initiative (We-Fi).

Abbreviations

ACIAR	Australian Center for International Agricultural Research
ADB	Asian Development Bank
AIIB	Asian Infrastructure Investment Bank
BCW	Business Coalition for Women
CEDAW	Convention on the Elimination of All Forms of Discrimination Against Women
CEO	chief executive officer
COVID-19	coronavirus disease
DHS	Demographic Health Surveys
DMC	developing member country
ECD	early childhood development
FEMM	Forum Economic Ministers' Meeting
FWCC	Fiji Women's Crisis Center
GBV	gender-based violence
HIES	Household Income and Expenditure Surveys
IDB	Inter-American Development Bank
LBT	lesbian, bisexual, and transgender
LBTQI	lesbian, bisexual, transgender, queer, and intersex
MICS	Multiple Indicator Cluster Surveys
MSMEs	micro, small, and medium-sized enterprises
NEDC	Nauru Entrepreneurship Development Center
OECD	Organisation for Economic Co-operation and Development
Pacific RISE	Pacific Readiness for Investment in Social Enterprise
PIPSO	Pacific Islands Private Sector Organization
PPSDI	Pacific Private Sector Development Initiative
PSDI	Private Sector Development Initiative
PTI	Pacific Trade Invest

SBH	Samoa Business Hub
SDDirect	Social Development Direct
SDG	Sustainable Development Goal
SMEs	small and medium-sized enterprises
SPBD	South Pacific Business Development
STEM	science, technology, engineering, and mathematics
TTFT	Tugeda Tude fo Tumoro
TVET	technical and vocational education and training
UNCDF	United Nations Capital Development Fund
UNCTAD	United Nations Conference on Trade and Development
UNHLP	United Nations High Level Panel
VAWG	violence against women and girls
WIBDI	Women in Business Development Inc.
WBL	Women, Business and the Law

Executive Summary

Promoting women's economic empowerment is a strategic operational priority of the Asian Development Bank (ADB), governments, and civil society in Pacific developing member countries. ADB's Strategy 2030 aims to support quality job-generation and higher value-added entrepreneurship opportunities for women as a way of narrowing gender gaps in the world of work. Micro, small, and medium-sized enterprises (MSMEs) play a huge role in economic development in the Pacific island countries and offer pathways to women's leadership and economic empowerment. This literature review summarizes the state of knowledge on women's economic empowerment in the Pacific developing member countries, focusing on women entrepreneurs and women-owned MSMEs in the formal and informal economies.

The report focuses on the ownership, formalization and expansion of women-owned businesses, the association between women's economic empowerment and violence against women and girls, and the effects of the coronavirus disease (COVID-19) pandemic. It provides recommendations for further research, policy and programmatic actions to increase women's economic participation and promote economic empowerment of women entrepreneurs and women-owned MSMEs in the Pacific. In total, 204 published papers and studies, as well as data from 11 quantitative databases, were reviewed and analyzed. Available evidence was synthesized under each research question where the strength of evidence was assessed and key evidence gaps highlighted. As anticipated, there is more extensive data and analytical resources on women's access to assets, services, networks, and opportunities than on women's voice and agency.

Status and Trends in Women's Economic Empowerment

Women are less likely to be in the labor force than men, and there are high levels of occupational concentration by sex, and gender pay gaps. Women's labor force participation is generally low, varying from 84% in Solomon Islands to 34% in Samoa (World Bank 2021a). Labor force participation is 30 percentage points lower for women in Fiji and Tuvalu compared to men, and more than 20 percentage points lower in the Marshall Islands and Samoa (ILO 2021b). This is despite most countries having close-to-gender parity in primary and secondary school enrollment. According to ILO (2014), working conditions are often poor, where women are at risk of sexual harassment and abuse and have little collective bargaining voice. Because of these dynamics, women are more likely to live in poverty. In Fiji, 64% of economically active women earned below the conservative poverty line for workers of F$4,000 per annum, compared with 38% to 40% of men (ADB 2014, cited in Michalena et al. 2020). Women with disabilities face additional barriers to accessing jobs, due to perceptions around their capacity to carry out paid work.

Women have less decision-making power than men. Many industries, including coastal fisheries and agriculture, are often perceived as male domains where women's decisions are unrecognized or unappreciated (Secretariat of the Pacific Community 2014). While women's representation in business leadership is favorable compared with global averages, it is far from representative. Women are less represented in senior leadership; on average, women hold 21% of board seats, 11% of board chair positions, and 13% of chief executive officer positions (Pacific Private Sector Development Initiative 2021).

Most Pacific island countries have laws that protect women's rights, however, there are gaps in legislation, and customary law acts as a barrier to women's economic empowerment. Apart from Palau and Tonga, all Pacific island countries have ratified the Convention on the Elimination of All Forms of Discrimination. Customary law often prohibits women from inheriting and owning land held under customary title. This prevents them from using land as a guarantee for loans that are needed to start or expand a business (ADB 2011). Across all countries, laws mandating equal renumeration for work of equal value and legislation on sexual harassment in the workplace are the least commonly enacted.

Pacific women carry unequal burdens of unpaid care work, and access to affordable and quality childcare is a key barrier for working parents particularly women. For example, across all age groups, women in Fiji spend approximately three times as much time on unpaid domestic chores and care work than men (Fiji Bureau of Statistics 2016 cited in Pacific Data Hub 2021a). Unpaid care work limits the time available for income-earning activities and diverts investment from business or training. An International Finance Corporation (IFC) (IFC 2019a) survey of more than 2,700 employees from the public and private sector in Fiji found that only 8% of parents with pre-school-age children use a childcare service.

Women have unequal access to training, credit, and job opportunities. Gender stereotypes influence educational choices and job opportunities (Michalena et al. 2020; Pacific Community 2017). Some job roles are considered culturally inappropriate such as the view that women will bring bad luck or a poor catch if they are on a fishing boat (Michalena et al. 2020). In Papua New Guinea, it is difficult for women to enforce contracts due to weaker bargaining power and cultural pressure to be submissive (Walton 2012). There are also some legal restrictions on women working in certain industries, or for work at night or work considered too dangerous (World Bank 2021d).

Productivity is lowered by poor infrastructure coverage and maintenance, particularly for women in remote areas. This includes electricity and digital technology coverage. Concerns over personal safety and a lack of reliable and affordable transport limits women's economic opportunities.

Pacific women, especially those in remote areas, have lower levels of access to digital technology than men despite strong evidence of its potential to improve business outcomes. Many women report that digital technology allows them to reach new markets, reduce travel costs, and order supplies (GSMA 2014). Mobile phones have enabled greater freedom for women (e.g., greater numbers of women fishing at night as it is considered safer) (Pacific Community 2019). Digital technology also allows business owners to provide records of savings and transactions, which improves the ability to secure loans (UNESCAP 2020b). But without digital skills training, women are at risk of being left behind. The main barriers to women's access to digital technologies are low awareness of potential benefits, price, and a perception that access would make their husbands suspicious.

Pacific women are more likely to experience the negative effects of climate change as they are less likely to have access to the resources and information they need to adapt and respond (UN Women 2014; ILO 2017b). Climate change is also affecting key industries that women rely on, such as agriculture, fisheries, and tourism (ADB 2019). For instance, women agricultural workers in Papua New Guinea have reported an increased burden of work due to reduced soil fertility and erosion, which has reduced yields and incomes (Mcleoda et al. 2018). There is a lack of evidence about women entrepreneurs in the green economy.

There are several policies that protect women's employment in formal and informal jobs, but there are weaknesses in the legislation and uneven enforcement. In 2012, Pacific Island leaders signed a Gender Equality Declaration and finance ministers adopted a Forum Economic Ministers' Meeting Action Plan, both of which include priorities for women's economic empowerment. However, legislation can reinforce paternalistic approaches; a 2021 study in Fiji found that women were portrayed as vulnerable or victims in 35 out of 55 small-scale fisheries policy instruments (Lawless et al. 2021).

Ownership, Formalization, and Expansion of Business

In the Pacific, it is mainly women who work in the informal economy, in low productivity jobs with limited capital and skill accumulation potential (ILO 2014; ADB 2019; UNCTAD 2020). Women tend to work in the lower segments of the informal work hierarchy as homeworkers and unpaid family workers. Informal work often gives Pacific women greater flexibility to juggle their multiple responsibilities, including unpaid care work. Other reasons for remaining in the informal economy include lack of awareness of the process of formalization; lack of convenient access to regulatory authorities in remote areas; difficulties in accessing opportunities and markets due to geographical remoteness and lack of infrastructure; demands from family and community for money when in paid work; and compliance costs associated with labor regulations, taxes, and license fees (ADB 2018; UNCTAD 2020). Low levels of labor force participation and concentration in the informal economy limit women's access to social protection, including in older age, reinforcing their vulnerability and poverty.

Women's entrepreneurship is common in the Pacific region, especially in family businesses, however, female ownership remains most prevalent in smaller and informal firms. There is a majority-women ownership in 24.3% of all small-sized firms in the Pacific, 38.8% in all medium-sized firms, and 23.2% in all large-sized firms (IFC 2019 cited in ADB 2019). A total of 90.2% of women-owned MSMEs are in the informal sector (IFC 2019 cited in ADB 2019). Regionally, women are typically concentrated in industries that experience intense competition and generate lower returns such as agriculture, retail, restaurants, hospitality and tourism, and handicrafts (ADB 2018e cited in ADB 2019). There is some evidence that women in the Pacific are increasingly becoming entrepreneurs (Mohanty 2011; Narsey 2011 cited in Walton 2012; Government of the Cook Islands 2012; Lambeth et al. 2014; FAO 2019; UNESCAP 2020a). Women-owned businesses—which mostly operate as MSMEs—tend to employ more women than large (mostly male-owned) firms (ADB 2019).

There is limited evidence in the literature on how women-owned micro, small, and medium-sized enterprises in the formal economy are expanding. An UNCTAD survey of 82 participants in Kiribati found that women are responding to emerging demand for products and services, attending government training and participating in women expos.

There is strong evidence on the wide-ranging set of barriers that women-owned MSMEs and women entrepreneurs experience in the expansion and formalization of their businesses:

- **Social norms.** Culturally, women are largely not expected to become successful in business, and often have no option but to balance paid and unpaid care work responsibilities, which can restrict their mobility and productivity and confine them to lower incomes. However, there is some variation among the Pacific island countries in terms of restrictive social norms. For instance, in Tonga, there is a growing acceptance of women's entrepreneurship, but this is not the case in Samoa and Fiji, where there is still a lack of entrepreneurial culture for women (IFC 2010; IFC 2016; Upadhyaya and Rosa 2019). In Melanesia, gifting other community members (*wantok*) can disincentivize savings and act as a barrier to starting and sustaining a business. Women are less likely than men to withstand pressure to help family members (Meleisea et al. 2015; ADB 2018a).

- **Access to commercial finance.** Women-owned businesses experience greater barriers in accessing finance than men-owned businesses. Many Pacific women have limited ownership of private land and therefore it cannot be used to secure collateral for commercial finance (Hedditch and Manuel 2010a; 2010b). Other barriers to accessing finance include a lack of financial expertise and experience, high equity requirements, high interest rates, complex documentation requirements, fewer business networks, a lack of confidence, lower rates of mobile phone ownership, and poor digital literacy (Nagarajan 2021).

- **Business literacy, skills, and access to information.** Studies from Fiji, Papua New Guinea, and Samoa suggest that many women have lower business literacy and skills than men (Hedditch and Manuel 2010a; ADB 2015; IFC 2016; FAO 2019). In Papua New Guinea, ADB (2015) found that women are 25% less financially literate than men. Women also often have less access to timely and reliable market information.

- **Voice and accountability.** Women often have greater difficulty in accessing the justice system for resolving commercial disputes and are less likely to complain (IFC 2010; ADB 2015; ADB 2018a). This makes women more vulnerable to corruption (UNDP and UNODC 2020).

Impact investment is nascent in the Pacific. The gender-lens investment that does occur is defined narrowly as investment in women-owned enterprises and tends to over-prioritize investor needs. There is weak evidence about how women entrepreneurs are using digital technologies to crowdfund and seek out peer-to-peer funding.

There is less information on the opportunities that access to finance, digital technology, and other resources brings to women's businesses. There is some evidence on the positive outcomes that women's access to finance can bring, such as greater involvement in household spending, establishment and growth of women-owned businesses, and increased savings (Pacific Women Shaping Pacific Development 2017; Pacific Financial Inclusion Program 2020). Supply-side initiatives in the region include banks' expansion of access to credit via a wider range of lending products, more flexibility in eligibility criteria, lower rates of interest, and more flexible repayment schemes that are more suited to women entrepreneurs (Pacific Islands Forum Secretariat 2021). Various Pacific island countries have progressed toward a secured transaction framework; simplification and certainty because of the framework has encouraged women to take out loans. Demand-side initiatives include business and financial literacy training, mentoring, and microfinance support. Less evidence was found on access to digital technology but some evidence indicates that once women gain access to information and communication technology tools and services, they tend to use them equally as or more than men (ADB 2019).

Many Pacific island countries continue to have a weak enabling environment for promoting women's business and entrepreneurship, but digital processes are the most widely cited positive change.
For example, in Tonga, a business license can be applied for online. Applying online is quicker and avoids transport costs and fees, which are particularly burdensome for time-poor women, although it does rely on an internet connection (Pacific Women Shaping Pacific Development 2017). Women in the Pacific are less likely to have access to a computer or a smartphone and are less likely to have the digital literacy skills to use online platforms. Few Pacific island countries have policy or legislative frameworks that explicitly support or actively promote gender-responsive procurement.

There are a wide variety of business networks in the Pacific, but due to capacity and funding gaps, their remit is mainly around building assets, capabilities, and opportunities for women. There is little evidence of seeking transformational changes that address unequal power relations and systemic institutional, legal, and societal barriers for women. With small budgets, little capacity, and few staff, these networks tend to provide business and financial training to women (ADB 2018a). Women in Business Development, Inc. (WIBDI) in Samoa has achieved considerable success through promoting and supporting organic certification of agricultural enterprises. There are also networks at the local level where women are supporting each other in business; and in Kiribati, these small groups are increasingly consulted by Island Councils (UNCTAD 2020). Market associations are making improvements to market facilities and security (Pacific Islands Forum Secretariat 2020).

Association Between Women's Economic Empowerment and Violence Against Women and Girls

Violence against women and girls is prevalent in the Pacific region, causing significant harm, and high costs to business. Women in the region experience various forms of violence, including economic abuse and reproductive coercion from partners. In the Marshall Islands, 27% of ever-partnered women reported that their partners either took their earnings or refused to give them money (ADB 2019). Women also experience violence at work from colleagues and customers, and on their way to and from work. Marketplaces can be particularly unsafe. For example, a United Nations (UN) Women (2011) scoping study of the markets in Port Moresby, Papua New Guinea, found that 22% of female market vendor respondents experienced more than one incidence of sexual violence at work in the last 12 months. Violence also has high costs for business. An International Finance Corporation (IFC) survey of 1,200 employees in Solomon Islands found that lost work time because of violence totals 2 working weeks per year per employee due to feeling distracted, tired, unwell, or being late or absent (IFC 2019c).

There is mixed evidence about whether women's increasing income correlates with increased intimate partner violence. In Vanuatu, women who have their own source of income are around 150% more likely to experience physical and sexual violence than those who do not (ADB 2019). On the other hand, a survey of 3,538 households in Fiji found that women's economic empowerment can be a key pathway to support women to leave a violent relationship (FWCC 2013). Increased income can also lessen stress and tension in the household, and result in more amicable husband–wife relationships (Vunisea and Fleming 2019). Few studies address violence against women and girls and women's economic empowerment interconnections for women-owned MSMEs and women entrepreneurs in the Pacific.

Civil society, businesses, and women's business networks have all played a key role in raising awareness of and helping to prevent violence against women and girls in the Pacific region. For instance, the Fiji Women's Rights Movement initiated the "Not OK: Stop Sexual Harassment" campaign, which was part of a successful lobby to ratify the International Labour Organization (ILO) Convention 190—an international treaty on violence and harassment at work—making Fiji one of only 25 countries globally where C190 is ratified (Center for Women's Global Leadership 2021). The Papua New Guinea Business Coalition for Women (BCW) has developed resources, policies, and workplace practices for companies, and provides training and support (Papua New Guinea BCW 2021). The Meri Seif (Women Safe) bus scheme in Papua New Guinea has provided an estimated 141,902 women and girls a safe journey to their job, school, or the market (Pacific Women Shaping Pacific Development 2021c).

Early signs suggest that interventions that partner with the private sector are effective in addressing violence experienced by women workers. Fifteen large companies in Solomon Islands have committed to introducing policies for respectful workplaces under the Waka Mere project with an IFC survey showing much lower levels of acceptance of violence among Waka Mere employees than previous studies (IFC 2019c, Pacific Shaping Pacific Development Women 2021c).

Effects of the Coronavirus Disease (COVID-19) Pandemic

Women entrepreneurs, women-owned micro, small, and medium-sized enterprises, and women workers have been particularly negatively affected. Global travel restrictions have severely affected women-owned MSMEs that sell to tourists (COVID-19 Response Gender WG 2020). International migrants have been unable to travel home, and do not qualify for many government benefits in their host country (Center for Humanitarian Leadership 2020; Howes 2020). There is strong evidence that women-owned MSMEs have been worse affected than male-owned MSMEs. In July 2020, Pacific Trade Invest (PTI) found that 41% of women-owned businesses had temporarily closed compared to 29% of male-owned businesses (PTI 2020). By the end of 2021, 20% of female-owned businesses had temporarily closed compared to 8% of male-owned businesses (PTI 2021). More recently established women-owned MSMEs and businesses with more than five employees have been more negatively impacted than those that have been in business for a longer period and those with fewer employees (CIPE 2021).

There is mixed evidence on who has been hardest hit—women entrepreneurs in the formal economy or the informal economy. A survey of 144 women entrepreneurs in Papua New Guinea found that women with registered businesses experienced more hardship compared to women with unregistered businesses (CIPE 2021). This could be because informal businesses have more flexibility in business operations. However, in Fiji, female market vendors and farmers tend to have few savings, which are not enough to sustain a short-term downturn in income (COVID-19 Response Gender WG 2020).

Women entrepreneurs and women-owned micro, small, and medium-sized enterprises have also been negatively affected by increases in unpaid care work responsibilities. School closures and the need to look after and educate children at home, coupled with caregiving for sick family members, have reduced the time that women can spend in managing a business (ADB 2020b; UNESCAP 2020a).

Gendered barriers in access to finance have worsened the impact of COVID-19 for women entrepreneurs. The PTI business monitor survey found that 65% of women-owned businesses needed financial support at the time of the survey (July 2020) compared to 49% of male-owned businesses (PTI 2020).

Women entrepreneurs have been using digital technologies to lessen the impacts of COVID-19, but the pandemic has widened the digital gender gap. In Fiji, a Facebook page created in April 2020 gained over 114,000 members (mainly women) within 2 weeks. It serves as a platform for non-cash trading and bartering of household and work-related items, and some women entrepreneurs are shifting to producing face masks and doing home delivery (Pacific Islands Forum Secretariat 2020). Women have less access to digital technologies and have fewer digital skills than men, limiting their access to accurate information on COVID-19 (Pacific Women Shaping Pacific Development 2020).

There are some promising examples of COVID-19 support, but evidence is not yet available on their impact. National government stimulus packages for women-owned MSMEs tend to prioritize credit. For instance, the government stimulus package in the Federated States of Micronesia includes credit to at least 200 MSMEs with 50% of the loan amount to women-owned MSMEs (ADB 2020b). These types of loans tend to require businesses to be registered, excluding the many women-owned businesses in the informal economy. Some Pacific governments are reaching the informal economy through one-off payments, but the amounts are often too low (Pacific Islands Forum Secretariat 2020).

Key Evidence Gaps

A range of large regional development partner programs addressing women's economic empowerment in the Pacific are ongoing or have recently closed, although independent published evaluations are not currently available for all. These include the Department of Foreign Affairs and Trade's (DFAT) Pacific Women Shaping Pacific Development (2012–2021), DFAT's Market Development Facility (2011–2022), ADB's Private Sector Development Initiative (2007 to present), DFAT's Pacific Readiness for Investment in Social Enterprise (2016–2021), and the Markets for Change (2014–2020) funded by DFAT and implemented by UN Women and the United Nations Development Programme. Lessons learned include (i) strategic partnerships with the government and the private sector can lead to improvements in women's working conditions, (ii) local groups can positively disrupt harmful social norms, and (iii) the "family teams" approach can lead to more gender-equitable farming practices (Mikhailovich and Pamphilon 2016). For financial inclusion initiatives, it is important to engage with male leaders to build support, and mobile banking services can increase women's independence, privacy, control, and decision-making.

The strength of the thematic evidence is mixed and there are gaps for specific Pacific island countries and for certain methodologies. Evidence is strongest for the status and trends in women's economic empowerment in the Pacific, particularly on women's access to assets, services, and opportunities. Evidence is weaker for how climate change is affecting women's economic empowerment. There is strong evidence on the key barriers, status, and trends impacting women-owned MSMEs, but no evidence on the risks for formalization of women-owned MSMEs. The strength of the evidence of the intersections between women's economic empowerment and violence against women and girls is medium, while there is limited evidence on the effectiveness of interventions. The strength of the evidence is also mixed on the impacts of COVID-19 on women-owned MSMEs, and there is no evidence on the effectiveness of government interventions. Most of the evidence available was for countries that have higher population numbers. Most studies used a mixed-methods approach but there was an absence of large-scale surveys.

Several countries have undertaken economic surveys to global standards, which include sex-disaggregated data. Examples are Demographic and Health Surveys, Household Income and Expenditure Surveys, Multiple Indicator Cluster Surveys, labor force surveys, and World Bank enterprise surveys. There is little information available on how data is informing policy on the economic empowerment of women entrepreneurs and women-owned MSMEs.

Conclusions and Recommendations

The literature indicates the need to create economic opportunities for women that increase agency, and lead to improvements in well-being and status, building on what has been learned previously. It is equally important to support livelihoods for women in both the informal and formal economies (Hearle et al. 2019). Digital technologies have huge potential to improve business outcomes for women, through reaching new markets and accessing financial services. Yet they also pose new risks with women being left behind and exposed to new forms of violence and exploitation. The following is a summary of research, policy, and program recommendations based on prioritization for furthering women's economic empowerment in the Pacific.

Recommendations on Areas for Further Research

High Priority

- Status and trends of women-owned MSMEs and women entrepreneurs in islands where there are smaller populations;

- Women's economic empowerment status and trends for women from groups that have historically been marginalized more than others such as women with disabilities, sexual and gender minorities, ethnic and indigenous minority women, migrants, and those raising children on their own;

- Forms of support to women-owned businesses to become more resilient to climate change; and

- Effectiveness of COVID-19 government stimulus or support packages aimed at women-owned businesses and women entrepreneurs.

Medium Priority

- Incentives for business formalization and the entry points and mechanisms for expansion of formal businesses; and

- Interconnections between women's economic empowerment and violence against women and girls.

Lower Priority

- Strategies to influence social norms on women's roles in business; and

- Social protection options for workers in the lower segments of the informal economy, including women-owned informal MSMEs.

Policy Recommendations

High Priority

- Repeal legislation that prohibits women from certain types of work; and

- Regulators, such as central banks or banking authorities, to require sex-disaggregated data to be collected, reported and released publicly.

Medium Priority

- Ratify ILO Convention No. 190 on violence and harassment in the world of work and adopt and enforce sexual harassment legislation and policies in employment;

- Reform tax, finance, and licensing policies and systems to remove barriers and disincentives for women-owned businesses to formalize;

- Enact parental leave policies that can contribute to changing social norms;

- Introduce childcare policies to help women manage their own business in the informal economy, or those who want to return to, or stay at work after having children; and

- Promote and legislate equal renumeration for work of equal value in ways that suit national contexts.

Lower Priority

- Develop national regulatory frameworks for crowdfunding and peer-to-peer lending; and
- Incentivize gender responsive procurement processes in the public and private sector.

Program Recommendations

High Priority

- Encourage financial institutions to accept non-land assets as collateral and increase uptake of secured transaction frameworks;
- Work with national statistical agencies and designers of international surveys to improve the quality of existing surveys, and include sex-disaggregated questions;
- Develop and implement targeted measures to help self-employed women restart their businesses that have collapsed or are in "survival mode" because of challenges associated with the COVID-19 pandemic; and
- Invest in evidence-based programming that aims to shift harmful social norms that sustain violence against women and girls in the world of work, with a focus on women entrepreneurs and women-owned MSMEs.

Medium Priority

- Building on good practice and experience in the Pacific, work with banks to adjust their risk assessment criteria in favor of MSMEs and informal businesses, and ensure financial products and services are adapted to women clients;
- Improve access to and understanding of regulations and official procedures;
- Support in-country stakeholders to disrupt social norms that act as barriers to women's business, and work with men and boys to support women's economic empowerment;
- Develop the unpaid and paid care provider economy and infrastructure, such as supporting quality and affordable care services;
- Fund women's business networks and raise their capacity to engage in activities that are more diverse; and
- Leverage digital access and increase access to mobile phones for women, accompanied with skills building on digital literacy, and scale up promising initiatives.

Lower Priority

- Partner with the private sector to address violence experienced by women workers in the formal sector;
- Mobilize capital for women-owned businesses by encouraging financial intermediaries to increase the percentage of loans meeting 2X Challenge criteria designed to increase investment in women in developing countries; and
- Work with technical and vocational education and training institutions and other educational institutions to increase availability and accessibility of business and entrepreneurship courses for women and increase their capacity to become adequately equipped for work.

1 Introduction

Woman standing in front of fishing boat.

Promoting women's economic empowerment is a strategic operational priority for the Asian Development Bank (ADB) and for its developing member countries (DMCs). ADB's Strategy 2030 aims to support quality jobs generation and higher value-added entrepreneurship opportunities for women to narrow gender gaps in the world of work. Micro, small, and medium-sized enterprises (MSMEs) in both the formal and informal economy play a huge role in economic development in Pacific island countries and offer pathways to women's leadership and economic empowerment.

ADB has prepared this literature review to provide an up-to-date summary of the state of knowledge on women's economic empowerment in the Pacific, focusing on women entrepreneurs and women-owned MSMEs in the formal and informal economies. The research, data analysis, and writing of this report have been funded by the Women Entrepreneurs Finance Initiative. The report summarizes the strength of the evidence base and highlights key evidence gaps. It includes the following subtopics related to women's economic empowerment:

(i)   Links with violence against women and girls, focusing on women entrepreneurs and women-owned MSMEs;

(ii) Barriers, challenges, and successes of women in formalizing businesses or in moving from micro or small enterprises to medium-sized enterprises; and

(iii) Effects of the coronavirus disease (COVID-19) pandemic on women entrepreneurs and women-owned MSMEs and effectiveness of government stimulus or support packages in mitigating the pandemic's impact.

Findings from the literature review will inform further research and data collection, as well as provide data and an evidence base to inform ADB, Pacific governments, and development partners designing and undertaking interventions in this area. This report begins with a brief description of the methodology used (Section 2) before summarizing key findings (Section 3). Finally, the conclusions and recommendations for research, policy making, and program design are presented (Section 4).

Methodology

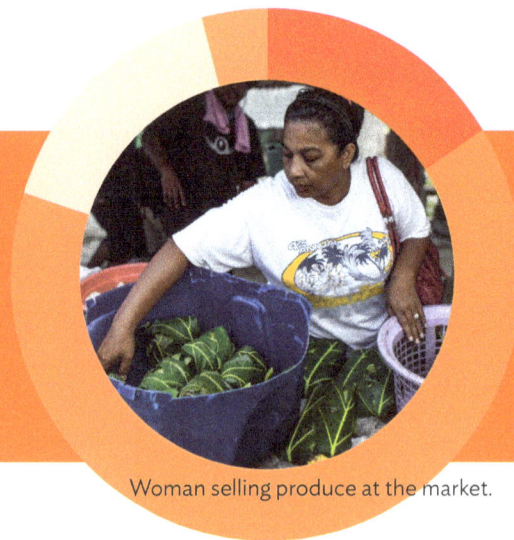

Woman selling produce at the market.

Conceptual Framework

Women's economic empowerment is about women having the ability to succeed and advance economically, and the power to make and act on economic decisions to enhance their well-being and position in society (Calder et al. 2020). In this study the Calder (2019) cited in Hearle et al. (2020) framework for women's economic empowerment is used (Figure 1). The three domains are:

- **Women's access to economic assets, services, networks, and opportunities.** Access to and control over financial, physical, technological, and knowledge-based assets, networks, services, and opportunities, including access to capital, training and mentoring, business opportunities, and markets.

- **Enabling environment.** Policies, laws, legislation, rules and regulations at the market and state level, and norms—exercised primarily at the household or family and community levels but also present in formal institutions—that mediate women's access to and control over economic assets within their household, businesses, community, and local economy.

- **Women's voice and agency.** Individual capabilities, sense of entitlement, self-esteem, and self-belief to make economic decisions, and the ability to organize with others to enhance economic activity and rights.

Figure 1: Women's Economic Empowerment Conceptual Framework

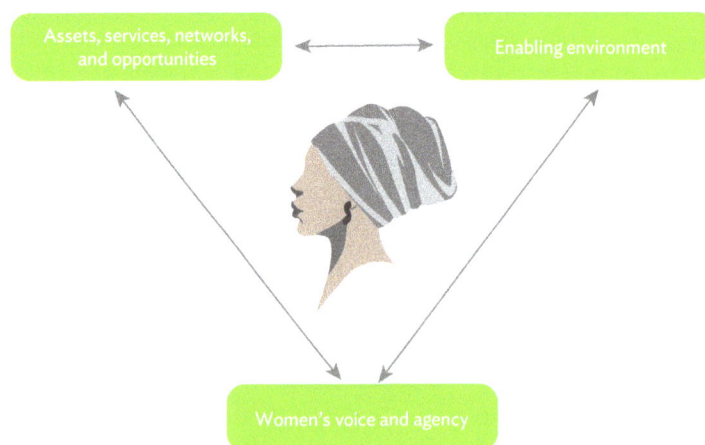

Assets, services, networks, and opportunities

Enabling environment

Women's voice and agency

Source: Calder (2019) cited in Hearle et al. (2020).

The literature review is guided by five key research questions:

(i)   What are the status and trends of women's economic empowerment in the Pacific?

(ii)   How are women owning, formalizing, and expanding their businesses?

(iii)   What is the association between women's economic empowerment and violence against women and girls for women entrepreneurs and women-owned MSMEs in the Pacific?

(iv)   How has the COVID-19 pandemic affected women's economic empowerment in the Pacific?

(v)   What are the key evidence gaps on women's economic empowerment in the Pacific?

Each research question includes some more detailed research questions to draw out the evidence further (see Appendix 1).

Methodological Approach

Three principal stages were applied to the literature review.

Stage 1: Data Scanning

In total, 204 publications and data from 11 quantitative databases were included in the review. A rapid review of the evidence on women's economic empowerment in the Pacific was conducted, focusing on women entrepreneurs and women-owned MSMEs in the formal and informal economies.

- **Search strategy.** Quantitative data and trends on women's economic empowerment in the Pacific were sought using a range of datasets.[1] Using search terms, relevant evidence and studies on Google, Google Scholar, and journals were gathered via the EBSCO research database. Papers were identified through professional networks. Searches were undertaken between October and December 2021.

- **Inclusion and exclusion criteria.** The literature review includes documents published from 2010 onward, in English language, and covers regional and country documents for ADB DMCs.[2] Regional reports relating to Asia and the Pacific and the Indo-Pacific region were excluded from the study. The literature review covered preprints, peer-reviewed, and gray literature.[3]

Stage 2: Evidence Mapping

Article titles and key details were mapped into an Excel matrix template. After scanning the initial evidence, the reviewers independently screened the citations and removed any duplicate studies and/or studies that did not meet the inclusion criteria.

---

[1]   Data sets used are the Pacific Data Hub, Demographic and Health Surveys, OECD's Social Institutions and Gender Index, United Nations country data, Asia-Pacific SDG Data Portal, Pacific DMC statistics offices, United Nations Children's Fund's Multiple Indicator Cluster Survey, United Nations Human Development Data, International Labour Organization Department of Statistics, the World Bank Gender Data Portal, World Bank Enterprise Surveys, World Economic Forum Global Gender Gap Index, MSME Finance Gap, and the Women Business and the Law database.

[2]   Countries covered by this report are the Cook Islands, the Federated States of Micronesia, Fiji, Kiribati, the Marshall Islands, Nauru, Niue, Palau, Papua New Guinea, Samoa, Solomon Islands, Tonga, Tuvalu, and Vanuatu.

[3]   Gray literature refers to materials and research produced by organizations outside of the traditional commercial or academic publishing and distribution channels.

Relevant text from documents was then coded into the Excel document, with columns that responded broadly to the research questions. Information such as author, year, title of publication, country, type of evidence, methods used, research participants, and sample size, together with any concerns about bias, were also recorded. Independent data checks on a random selection of evidence were conducted to check the quality of the data inputted.

Stage 3: Report Writing

Available evidence was synthesized under each research question and is summarized in Section 3. Drawing on the findings, conclusions, and recommendations are outlined in Section 4.

3 Key Findings

Woman learning to sew.

Status of and Trends in Women's Economic Empowerment

How has women's access to assets, services, and opportunities, as well as voice and agency, changed?

Women's labor force participation is generally low across the Pacific island countries, varying from 84% in Solomon Islands to 34% in Samoa in 2019 (Figure 2) (World Bank 2021b). Overall, rates of female labor force participation in the region have increased slightly from 51% in 1999 to 55% in 2019.[4] In Papua New Guinea, the rate fell from 72% in 1999 to 48% in 2019 (World Bank 2021b).

Figure 2: Female Labor Participation Rate (% Female Population Ages 15+)

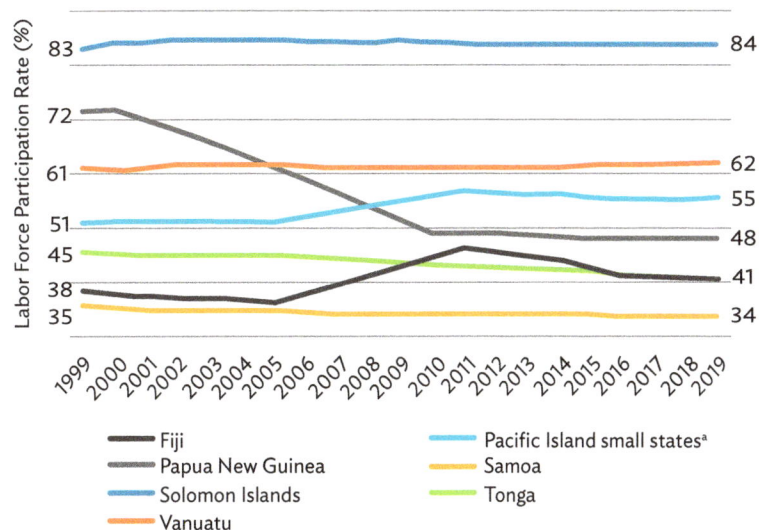

Legend:
- Fiji
- Papua New Guinea
- Solomon Islands
- Vanuatu
- Pacific Island small states[a]
- Samoa
- Tonga

[a] Pacific Island small states include the following countries: Fiji, Kiribati, the Marshall Islands, the Federated States of Micronesia, Nauru, Palau, Samoa, Solomon Islands, Tonga, Tuvalu and Vanuatu.

Note: Data is from modeled International Labour Organization estimates.

Source: World Bank (2021b).

---

4   Not all countries were included due to a lack of data.

Women's labor force participation is lower than that of men across the region. The gender disparity in labor force participation was more than 30 percentage points in Fiji and Tuvalu and more than 20 percentage points in the Marshall Islands and Samoa (Figure 3) (ILO 2021b). Papua New Guinea and Solomon Islands have the smallest gaps at 4 percentage points or less.

Figure 3: Female and Male Employment Rates Across Pacific Island Countries

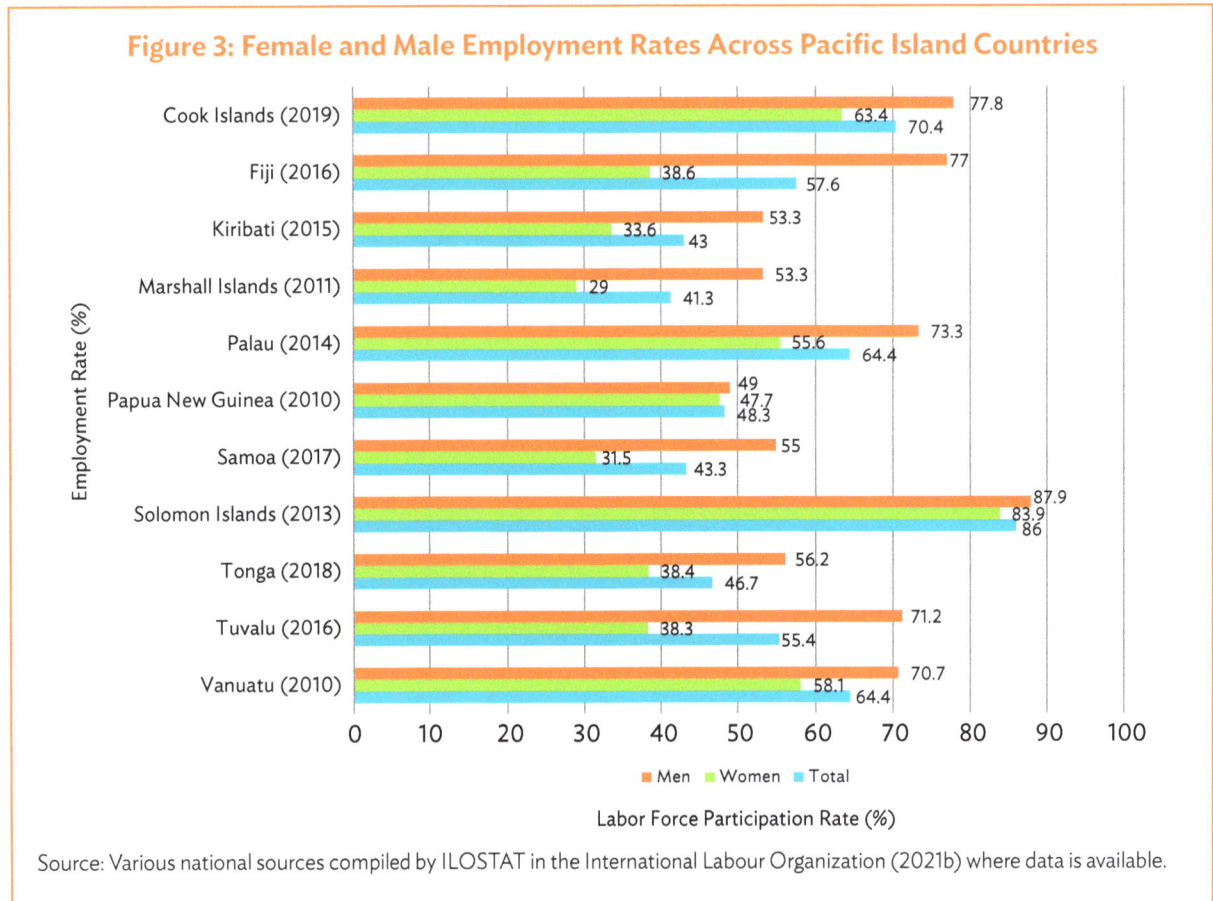

Source: Various national sources compiled by ILOSTAT in the International Labour Organization (2021b) where data is available.

Women are overrepresented in the informal economy, particularly in micro and small enterprises that require little capital to start or maintain (ADB 2018a). Labor markets in the Pacific have large informal and subsistence economies and high rates of vulnerable employment, wherein women, including women who are contributing family workers, are overrepresented (Asia Foundation 2021). Women are overrepresented in vulnerable employment (Figure 4) partly because of a limited number of formal sector jobs in the Pacific, most of which are in the public service (Pacific Islands Forum Secretariat 2020). Women in the informal economy have no social protection, no access to paid maternity leave, and no job protection (Asia Foundation 2021; Pacific Community 2017).

Young people are less likely to participate in the formal economy. In 2017, young women faced the highest unemployment rates in all Pacific island countries, except for the Cook Islands (ILO 2017b). In the Marshall Islands, Nauru, and Tuvalu, there are youth unemployment rates above 50%, as shown in Figure 5 (ILO 2017a).

There are high levels of occupational concentration by sex in the Pacific. Women are overrepresented in the undervalued "female" occupations in the service sector (including domestic work and unpaid care work), tourism, garment industry, food processing, health, and social work (Asia Foundation 2021; ILO 2014).

Figure 4: Vulnerable Employment in Selected Pacific Island Countries, by Sex

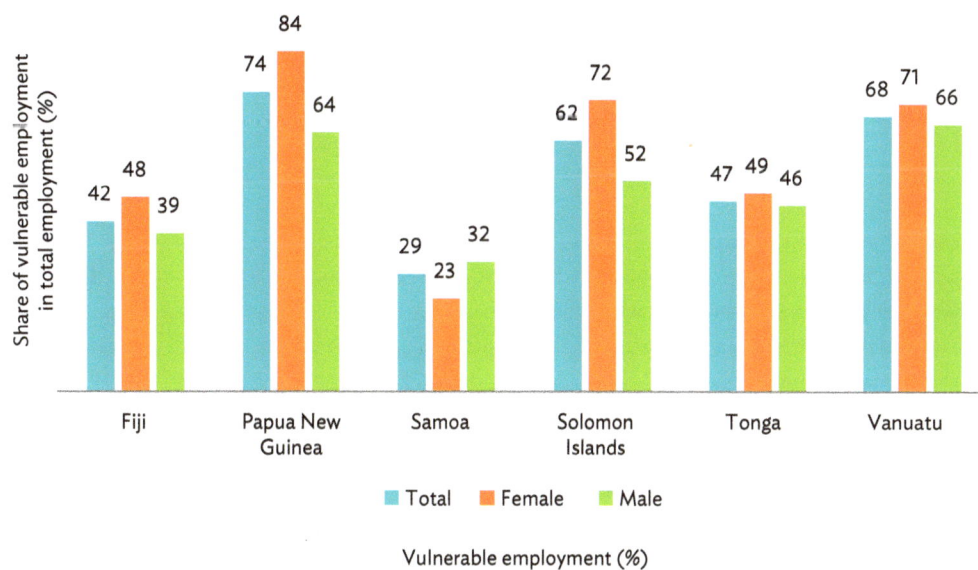

Note: Data is from modeled International Labour Organization (ILO) estimates, derived from ILOSTAT database.
Source: ILO (2021b). Data from 2019.

Figure 5: Unemployment Rates for Young People (15–24 Years Old), by Sex

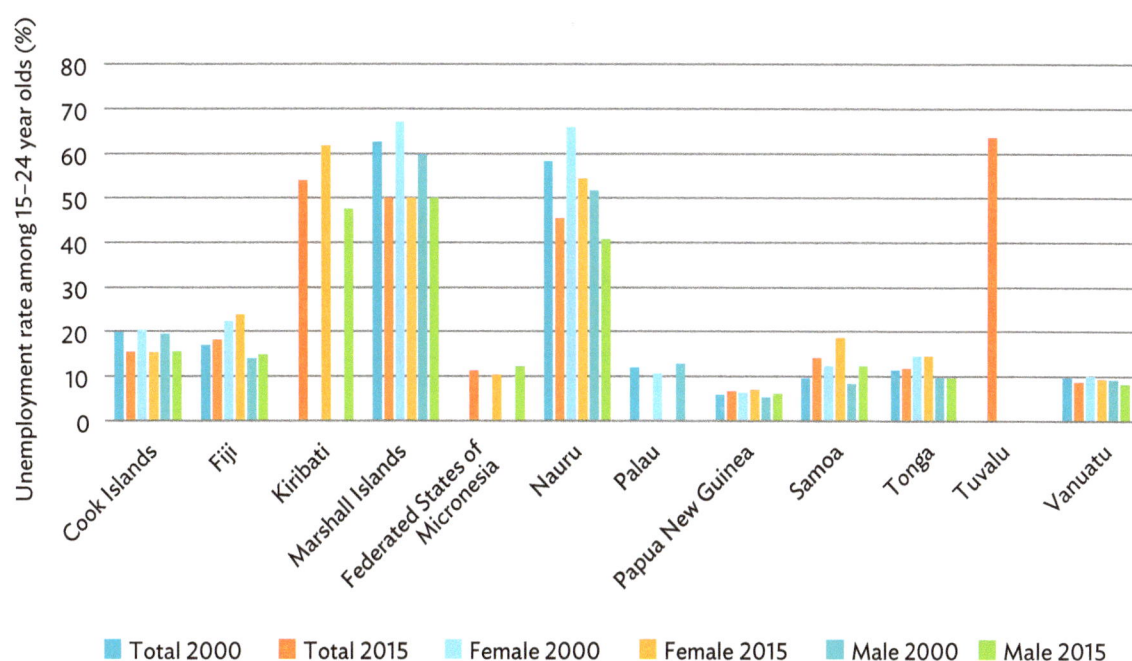

Note: Data for the Cook Islands, Kiribati, the Marshall Islands, Nauru, Palau, Papua New Guinea, Samoa, Tonga, and Tuvalu are drawn from the Secretariat of the Pacific Community (SPC 2017) cited in ADB and ILO (2017a).
Source: ADB and ILO (2017a).

For example, women represent 81% of nurses in the Western Pacific (Boniol et al. 2019).[5] In Kiribati, 26% of women are employed in both formal and informal jobs in the manufacturing sector,[6] making it the top employment sector for women, whereas only 5.7% of men are employed in manufacturing (UNCTAD 2020). The manufacturing sector in Kiribati has the highest female intensity of labor in the country at 77%. In these female-dominated sectors, wages are typically lower, working conditions are poor, there are high levels of sexual harassment and abuse, and workers have little collective bargaining voice (ILO 2014). Some female-dominated sectors, particularly manufacturing, are at risk of future streamlining of the workforce because of potential automation and digitalization (Asia Foundation 2021).

There is growth in women's employment in sectors such as wholesale and retail trade; financial and insurance activities; real estate, business, and administrative activities; education; and human health and social work activities across the Pacific. Between 1991 and 2017, women's employment in these sectors grew by an average of at least 5% a year (ADB 2019). Significant growth in women's participation in tourism and information technology-enabled services is also expected, which is a positive trend (ADB 2019).

Men tend to dominate the formal jobs in major economic sectors while women are more likely to work in informal or less lucrative roles. In agriculture and fisheries, men tend to hold most of the jobs in the formal economy, with women more involved in the informal economy, such as processing, marketing, and selling goods at markets (Asia Foundation 2021). In 2011 in the Marshall Islands, Solomon Islands, and Tonga, 60% of the administrative and clerical staff in government fisheries departments are women, compared to 18% of the total staff (Tuara and Passfield 2011). Many of these industries, including coastal fisheries and agriculture, are often perceived as male domains. In these industries, decisions are often made by male community leaders, elders, and chiefs, and women's contributions are often not recognized or appreciated (Secretariat of the Pacific Community 2014). Despite this, Michalena et al. (2020) argue that women are gaining prominence in the Pacific marine economic sector in a variety of roles, such as catching and processing of fish and as fish merchants and managers in urban centers.[7]

Domestic trends in Pacific women's economic empowerment are often replicated when women migrate to other countries for work. Pacific women migrants work predominantly in housekeeping, caring, and service sector roles within regulated labor migration schemes for seasonal or temporary work in Australia or New Zealand (Asia Foundation 2021). Labor migration is an important economic strategy as women who migrate are paid more than those that stay (but less than men who migrate) and tend to get better jobs if they return. Despite this, women are underrepresented in seasonal work programs in Australia and New Zealand, where they represent only 17% of participants in either scheme (Curtain et al. 2016). Women migrants from Polynesia and Micronesia fare poorly in employment overseas; 45.2%, 41.7%, and 33.1% of women migrants from Polynesia, Micronesia, and Melanesia, respectively are not in the labor force (OECD 2010 cited in ILO 2017b).

While women's participation in business leadership is favorable compared with global averages, it is far from representative. According to a study by the Pacific Private Development Initiative (PPSDI 2021), on average, women hold 21% of board seats, 11% of board chair positions, 13% of chief executive officer (CEO) positions, and 34% of chief financial officer or chief operating officer positions (PPSDI 2021). In Vanuatu, for

---

[5]   The World Health Organization (WHO) Western Pacific region includes the following economies, some of which are not included in the scope of this literature review: American Samoa; Australia; Brunei Darussalam; Cambodia; the People's Republic of China; the Cook Islands; Fiji; French Polynesia; Guam; Hong Kong, China; Japan; Kiribati; the Lao People's Democratic Republic; Macau, China; Malaysia; the Marshall Islands; the Federated States of Micronesia; Mongolia; Nauru; New Caledonia; New Zealand; Niue; Northern Mariana Islands; Palau; Papua New Guinea; the Philippines; the Pitcairn Island; the Republic of Korea; Samoa; Singapore; Solomon Islands; Tokelau; Tonga; Tuvalu; Vanuatu; Viet Nam; and Wallis and Futuna.

[6]   This includes production of cigarettes, handicrafts, food and beverages, and garments.

[7]   The marine economic sector in the Pacific includes subsistence, commercial and industrial fisheries, transport and shipping, coastal and marine tourism, and deep-sea minerals.

example, women constitute 43% of the formal workforce, but hold only 7% of positions on the boards of state-owned enterprises (ADB and Asia Foundation 2018). A PPSDI (2021) study found that the business community offered greater opportunities for women's leadership than the political sphere. There was a higher proportion of women as board directors than women as members of Parliament in 13 of 14 countries included in the study, and higher proportion of women CEOs than members of Parliament in 10 Pacific Island countries.

Women, particularly those from socially excluded groups, are more likely to live in poverty. ADB (2014) found that 64% of economically active women in Fiji earned below the conservative poverty line for workers, compared with 38% to 40% of men. In the Cook Islands in 2011, households headed by women generally had lower household incomes than households headed by men. Among the single heads of households that live with their relatives, there was an 18% income gap between those headed by women and men (SPC 2012 cited in Pacific Community 2017). Limited evidence suggests that households headed by women; older women; widows; women with disabilities; lesbian, bisexual, and transgender (LBT) women; those living in remote areas; survivors of violence; and women living with family members who have a disability are often likely to experience financial hardship (Pacific Community 2017; UNFPA 2014). This affects women's ability to save, control assets, and open or expand businesses.

Access to education for girls has improved across the Pacific, with most countries close to achieving gender parity in primary and secondary school enrollment.[8] Despite this, there are still girls who do not receive secondary education, with the percentage of gross secondary school enrollment for girls particularly low in Melanesia at 42% for Fiji, 47% for Solomon Islands, and 55% for Vanuatu (Figure 6) (UNESCO Institute for Statistics 2021). Early pregnancy is a significant issue in the Pacific and contributes to lower retention and completion rates for girls due to barriers to sexual and reproductive health care (Clarke and Azzopardi 2017).

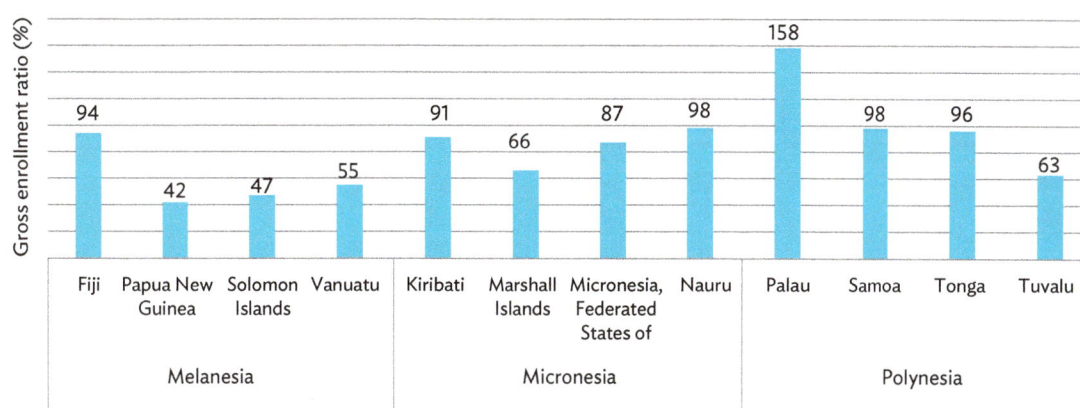

Figure 6: Gross Secondary School Enrollment, Female

Notes: The gross enrollment ratio can exceed 100% as it includes overage and underage students who repeat a grade or have early or late school entrance. The gross enrollment ratio is defined as the total enrollment in a specific level of education, regardless of age, expressed as a percentage of the eligible official school-age population corresponding to the same level of education in a given school year. https://uis.unesco.org/en/glossary-term/gross-enrolment-ratio. Data is included for the latest year available. Some countries are not shown due to a lack of data.

Source: United Nations Educational, Scientific and Cultural Organization (UNESCO) Institute for Statistics (2021).

---

[8]   Less educational progress has been reported for Melanesian countries (ADB 2011). AusAID (2011) cited in Walton (2012) reports that in Melanesia, only 45% of women receive secondary education compared to 88% in Micronesia and 83% in Polynesia.

Improved access to education has not yet translated into equal employment opportunities and control over the productive assets needed for business development (Pacific Community 2017). For instance, in Fiji, women account for nearly two-thirds of university students on tourism courses, yet they hold only a quarter of professional and managerial positions in the sector (Hamilton 2020). Instead, women in the formal tourism sector are concentrated in minimum-wage jobs, including reception and cleaning roles. Despite this, women are improving their skill levels more quickly than men. The average annual growth in employment in high-skilled occupations between 1991 and 2020 was 4.1% for women, compared to 3.2% for men (ADB 2019).[9]

What has changed in the enabling environment for women's economic empowerment, including policies and norms, that mediate women's access to and control over economic assets?

Table 1 shows that the Marshall Islands and Samoa have enacted since 2010 the greatest number of laws that protect women's economic rights, according to the indicators. In contrast, Vanuatu has not strengthened any of its laws. Across all countries, legislation specifically addressing intimate partner violence is the most common regulation that has been enacted, while laws mandating equal renumeration for work of equal value and legislation on sexual harassment in the workplace are the least commonly enacted. Many countries also have legislation mandating paid or unpaid maternity leave (i.e., Fiji, Kiribati, Papua New Guinea, Samoa, Solomon Islands, and Vanuatu) (ILO 2017b).

Table 1: Status of and Changes in Women's Economic Empowerment Legislation in the Pacific

Country	Does the law prohibit discrimination in employment based on gender?	Does the law mandate equal remuneration for work of equal value?	Is there legislation specifically addressing domestic violence?	Do men and women have equal ownership rights to immovable property?	Is there legislation on sexual harassment in the workplace?
Fiji	Yes	No	Yes*	Yes	Yes
Kiribati	Yes	Yes	Yes*	No	Yes*
Marshall Islands	Yes*	Yes*	Yes*	No	No
Federated States of Micronesia	No	No	Yes*	No	No
Palau	No	No	Yes*	No	No
Papua New Guinea	Yes	No	Yes*	Yes	No
Samoa	Yes*	No	Yes*	Yes	Yes*
Solomon Islands	No	No	Yes*	Yes	No
Tonga	No	No	Yes*	No	No
Vanuatu	No	No	Yes	No	No
Countries that have enacted gender equitable laws (%)	**50%**	**20%**	**100%**	**40%**	**30%**

Note: The asterisk (*) denotes a change since 2010 data.
Source: Women, Business and the Law Database, World Bank (2021d).

---

[9]   Highly skilled workers typically have higher specialized education and/or training and experience.

Despite some progress in legislation change, legal and policy barriers persist. This includes some restrictions on the type of jobs that women can take, such as in certain industries, or for work at night, or work considered too dangerous. In Vanuatu and Solomon Islands, women cannot work the same night hours as men. In Papua New Guinea, women are prohibited from working in jobs deemed dangerous in the same way as men. In Fiji, Papua New Guinea, and Solomon Islands, women are not able to work in some of the same industries as men (World Bank 2021d) [10] Unequal access to justice and the court system also present a barrier (ADB 2015). In some contexts, domestic workers,[11] who are predominantly women, are excluded from legislation (Pacific Women Shaping Pacific Development 2017).

All Pacific island countries have ratified the UN Convention on the Elimination of All Forms of Discrimination Against Women (CEDAW), except for Palau, which has signed but not ratified it, and Tonga.[12] The constitutions of many Pacific island countries prohibit discrimination on the grounds of sex and/or gender (Table 2) ADB (2018).

Despite the widespread ratification of CEDAW, customary law is recognized as valid in many countries, resulting in discriminatory practices that limit women's ability to engage in business or paid employment, which is contrary to CEDAW and constitutional commitments (ADB 2018; IFC 2010). This includes lack of land rights and cultural practices such as bride prices that restrict economic autonomy. The practice of bride price, where the groom or his family gives money, property, or other resources to the bride, reinforces women's economic dependence on their husbands as the bride price must be repaid if a woman leaves the marriage, which can also increase the risk of gender-based violence (Gerawa 2015).

Table 2: Constitutional Provisions Related to Women's Autonomy

Country	Constitution prohibits discrimination on the grounds of sex and/or gender?	Constitution recognizes customary law as a source of law?
Cook Islands	Yes	Yes
Federated States of Micronesia	Yes	Yes
Fiji	Yes	No
Kiribati	Partial	Yes
Marshall Islands	Yes	Yes
Palau	Yes	Yes
Papua New Guinea	Partial	Yes
Samoa	Yes	Yes
Solomon Islands	Yes	Yes
Tonga	No	No
Tuvalu	Partial	Yes
Vanuatu	Yes	Yes

Source: ADB (2018).

---

[10] In Papua New Guinea and Solomon Islands, women are not legally able to work in mining. In Papua New Guinea, women are prohibited from working in construction, energy, water, and transportation. In Papua New Guinea and Fiji, women are legally prohibited from working in factories in certain industries, World Bank (2021d).

[11] International Labour Organization (ILO) Convention 189 defines domestic work as "work performed in or for a household or households."

[12] Office of the United Nations High Commissioner for Human Rights (OHCHR). UN Treaty Body Database (accessed 14 December 2021).

Women's access to assets, finance, and services is limited by sociocultural norms.[13] The Pacific Financial Inclusion Program's assessment of the Women's and Girl's Access and Agency program in Fiji and Solomon Islands drew on key informant interviews, focus group discussions, and a survey of 400 women and girls (Pacific Financial Inclusion Program 2020). The assessment found that to open a bank account, socio cultural norms require women to seek their husband's permission, which is often not granted, especially when men are not involved in making the decision to open the account. The assessment also found that many women in remote areas in Fiji and Solomon Islands are not necessarily in control of decisions about the use of income they earn from market produce. Women reported hiding their earnings from their partners to keep money for household expenditure or to ensure that earnings were not spent on alcohol or cigarettes.

There is weak social protection for women in the private sector, particularly in the informal economy, where women are concentrated (ILO 2017b).[14] For example, only 2% of accounts in Solomon Islands National Provident Fund, which was established to provide retirement benefits and income to all citizens, are held by people working in the informal sector (ADB, 2013 cited in ADB 2015). In addition, 71% of accounts are held by men and there are restrictions on widows accessing their deceased husbands' savings. Unlike many provincial funds, the Solomon Islands National Provincial Fund offers a voluntary savings fund specifically for people who are self-employed, called youSave, available to anyone between the ages of 16 and 51.[15] Prevalence of paid parental leave and other benefits is low across the region (Table 3), with only Fiji offering paid maternity of at least 14 weeks (Women, Business and Law 2021). This paid maternity leave applies only to workers in the public sector, which means that women working in the commercial and informal sectors are not covered by these provisions (Pacific Community, 2017). Provision is particularly low in the Micronesia; and there is no paid maternity leave available in the Marshall Islands, the Federated States of Micronesia, and Palau.

Table 3: Availability of Maternity Benefits Across the Pacific Region

Subregion	Country	Is paid leave of at least 14 weeks available to mothers?	Length of maternity leave (days)?	Does the government administer 100% of maternity leave benefits?	Is there paid leave available to fathers?	Is dismissal of pregnant workers prohibited?
Melanesia	Fiji	Yes	98	No	Yes	Yes
	Papua New Guinea	No	0	No	No	No
	Solomon Islands	No	84	No	No	No
	Vanuatu	No	84	No	No	No
Micronesia	Kiribati	No	84	No	No	Yes
	Marshall Islands	No	0	No	No	No
	Federated States of Micronesia	No	0	No	No	No
	Palau	No	0	No	No	No
Polynesia	Samoa	No	28	No	Yes	Yes
	Tonga	No	0	No	No	No

Note: Some countries could not be included due to lack of data.
Source: World Bank (2021d).

There is legislation on domestic violence across the Pacific, except for the Federated States of Micronesia, where the legislation is in draft (ADB 2018). However, this legislation remains largely unenforced.

---

[13] Sociocultural norms can be defined as rules or expectations of behavior, expression, and values.
[14] ILO defines social protection as a set of policies and programs designed to reduce and prevent poverty and vulnerability throughout the life cycle.
[15] See Solomon Islands National Provident Fund. https://www.sinpf.org.sb/index.php/members-services/yousave.html.

What are the current key barriers to women's economic empowerment in Pacific island countries, and how do these barriers differ from the formal to the informal economy?

Many women are excluded from inheritance rights to customary lands, though both matrilineal and patrilineal inheritance systems exist (ADB 2019; Asia Foundation 2021). For example, 97% of land under customary tenure in Papua New Guinea is under patrilineal ownership (Drucza and Hutchens 2008 cited in Walton 2012). Women can use land owned by male relatives, such as for small-scale agriculture projects but they are often unable to register the land in their name, which prevents them from using it as a guarantee for loans, including those needed to start or expand a business (ADB 2011). For many women involved in agriculture, lack of land rights presents a barrier to pursuing further private sector and agricultural activities, especially those that are export-oriented (ADB 2019). This barrier particularly affects women in remote areas, where owning land is a crucial asset for entrepreneurship (ADB 2018). Even in traditionally matrilineal societies, women do not always have better property rights. For example, in provinces in Solomon Islands, matrilineal land tenure has not translated into decision-making about land use (ADB 2018). Large-scale developments, particularly mining and logging activities, have further affected women's participation in land decision-making as men often take over the responsibility and become trustees, signatories, and beneficiaries of royalty payments, often without proper consultation with women (Maetala 2008 cited in ADB 2018).

Unequal burden of unpaid work. In the Pacific, women carry unequal burdens of work, dedicating time to household, community, and church work alongside economic activities (Vunisea 2015; Hedditch and Manual 2010a). As women have become increasingly involved in economic activities, their traditional burden of unpaid work has not decreased (Thomas et al. 2021). Consistently across all age groups, Fijian women spend approximately three times as much time on domestic and care work than men (Figure 7).

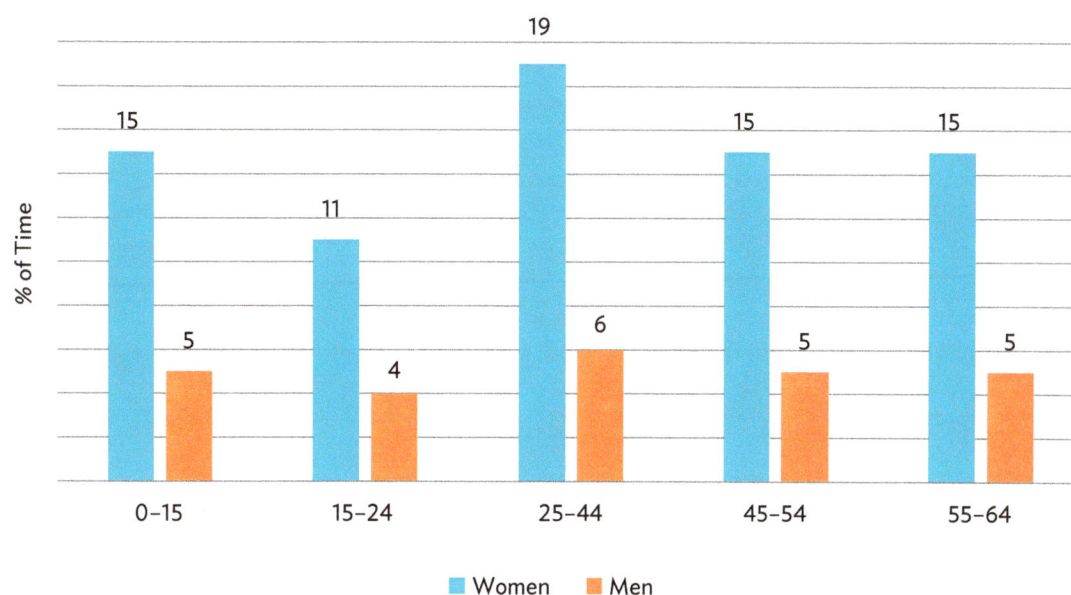

Figure 7: Time Spent on Domestic and Care Work in Fiji, Disaggregated by Sex and Age

Source: Fiji Bureau of Statistics' Employment and Unemployment Survey 2015-16; Collected by United Nations Statistics Division and reported by Pacific Data Hub (2021a).

Community and cultural obligations add additional time burdens for women, limiting the time available for income earning activity and diverting investment that may have otherwise been made in businesses or training. In an online survey of 92 women working in full- or part-time formal employment with an employer in Papua New Guinea, 45% of respondents identified the balancing of work and household responsibilities as a challenge. Qualitative research from the same research project revealed that domestic conflict can often arise when income activities are seen as impacting on women's domestic and unpaid care responsibilities (IWDA 2018a).

Access to affordable, quality childcare is a key barrier for working parents, particularly women. An International Finance Corporation (IFC) (2019a) survey of more than 2,700 employees from the public and private sectors in Fiji found that only 8% of parents with pre-school-age children included in the study use a childcare service. Formal childcare options are limited, with most parents relying on their partner (presenting a barrier to women reentering the workforce), other family members, or some unqualified services. The IFC survey (IFC 2019a) found that 82% of parents of school-age children reported that their care responsibilities impacted their work, for example, by being distracted at work or causing them to miss work, arrive late, or take a lower paid or part-time job. The report estimated that employers are losing over 11 working days per employees each year due to childcare responsibilities, with lost staff time costing as much as F$550,000 ($254,000 at the end of May 2019) a year in total. Of the 130 women who went on maternity leave in the 12 months preceding the survey, an average of 21% left their job within 12 months of returning to work.

Unequal access to training and job opportunities. Gender stereotypes influence the educational pathways women choose and the job opportunities available to them (Michalena et al. 2020; Pacific Community 2017). For example, while women play active roles in harvesting and selling, fisheries are considered male domains. This concentrates decision-making power in the hands of men. In addition, there are some roles that are considered culturally inappropriate for women. In some contexts, women are considered to bring bad luck and poor catch, if they are on a boat or near fishing activities (Michalena et al. 2020). A study in the Marshall Islands, Solomon Islands, and Tonga found that the belief that men are more suited to the fisheries sector, and a lack of awareness of the roles played by women, were key factors in limiting women's education and career choices in fisheries science and management (SPC 2014).

Unequal access to finance. Women in the Pacific are largely constrained by access to finance, especially those in remote areas where weak access to both public and private financial services is more pronounced. As shown in Table 4, the most common reasons why women do not access bank finance are high interest rates (34%), lack of security (19%), and inadequate loan amount (6%), although figures vary by country. An ADB survey found that women-owned firms faced 2.5 times more rejections than men-owned firms (Di Caprio and Beck 2017 cited in ADB 2019). These enterprises are less likely to receive loans from formal financial institutions such as banks, due to institutional bias, weaker credit histories or lack of credit history if they have not previously engaged with formal lenders, barriers to women holding identity documents needed to fulfill know-your-customer requirements, and fewer resources available as collateral for borrowing; they also tend to borrow for a shorter duration and with high interest rates (ADB 2018a; ADB 2019; Pacific Islands Forum Secretariat 2020; Sathye et al. 2014). In Kiribati, potential women borrowers are deterred by the lengthy application procedure and difficulties understanding the requirements for loans (UNCTAD 2020).

Women are disproportionately affected by high interest rates from financing institutions (ADB 2018a). High interest rates prevent 56% of women in Vanuatu from accessing bank finance (ADB 2015). Interest rates from informal moneylenders can be extortionate: 40% to 50% in Papua New Guinea, 8% to 21% in Samoa, and 50% to 250% every fortnight in Solomon Islands, with high repercussions for default (IFC 2016; Pacific Financial Inclusion Program 2020; UNESCAP 2020a).

Concerns have also been raised about the high levels of interest charged by microfinance providers. South Pacific Business Development (SPBD), which operates across the Pacific, charged interest rates that range from 24% to 27% per annum in Samoa (UNESCAP 2020a). Almost all SPBD's clients are women borrowing through a group lending system.

Women with disabilities face additional barriers to accessing jobs, due to perceptions that they are less capable of working or fulfilling their culturally ascribed roles as mothers, wives, and unpaid community workers (ILO 2014). A lack of investment in inclusive and accessible education remains a barrier to women and girls with disabilities (Pacific Islands Forum Secretariat 2020). Discrimination on the grounds of gender and ethnicity in the allocation of market stalls has also been reported in Fiji (Upadhyaya and Rosa 2019).

Societal expectations of gender roles also act as a barrier to women's economic empowerment. In Papua New Guinea, it is difficult for women to enforce contracts due to weaker bargaining power and cultural pressures to be submissive, which affects their income (Walton 2012). In a study conducted in Tonga, most women identified cultural expectations as their main barrier from entering the job market or starting a business (Cutura and Van Hooft 2009 cited in Walton 2012). Unequal access to educational and training opportunities and cultural traditions that prioritize men's role in leadership and decision-making are also a barrier to women's progress (ADB 2015; Pacific Private Sector Development Initiative 2021). In Samoa, business licensing requires personal attendance at a licensing office, which creates opportunities for personal and cultural bias to act as barriers (ADB 2018). An ADB (2018) study found that women business owners were particularly targeted for exploitation through this process, for example, through claims that business licenses or taxation had not been fully paid (when they had) or through the introduction of discretionary procedures that have complicated the process.

Economic productivity is restricted by poor infrastructure coverage and a lack of infrastructure maintenance, particularly for women in remote areas (Pacific Community 2017). This includes water, electricity, transport links, and digital technology coverage. Concerns over personal safety and a lack of reliable and affordable transport also limit women's access to jobs and markets. For instance, 55% of women in Port Moresby, Papua New Guinea experienced some form of sexual violence in market spaces in the previous year, which discouraged them from accessing markets and restricted their economic opportunities (UN Women 2014). Expensive market stall fees and poor market conditions, including space available for stock, shelter, drainage, toilet, and water facilities, are also cited as barriers (Upadhyaya and Rosa 2019; Vitukawalu et al. 2020).

How does climate change affect the status and trend of women's economic empowerment in the Pacific island countries?

As low-lying small island developing states, the Pacific island countries are becoming more vulnerable to climate change, and are already experiencing the effects of extreme weather events, including cyclones and typhoons, and slow-onset disasters, such as sea-level rise. In a survey of 377 households in Kiribati, 94% reported that they had been affected by environmental hazards over the last 10 years, with 81% affected by sea-level rise (Oakes et al. 2016). Women, especially those from other socially excluded groups, are at a higher risk of experiencing the negative effects of climate change as they are less likely to have access to the resources and information they need to adapt and respond, particularly as they are concentrated in more vulnerable, often informal, and lower paid employment (ILO 2017a; UN Women 2014). Box 1 gives an example of how Cyclone Pam affected female micro-entrepreneurs in Vanuatu.

Box 1: Women Entrepreneurs and Cyclone Pam

Approximately 3,600 female micro-entrepreneurs were affected when Cyclone Pam landed in Vanuatu in 2015. They lost an estimated 141,110 workdays or an average of 39 days each. A post-disaster needs assessment estimated that the additional unpaid work carried out by women to restore homes and gardens, fetch water and food, and take care of children while schools were closed, translated to lost earnings of a minimum of Vt432 million.

Source: SPC (2015) cited in Pacific Community (2017).

The region has experienced an increase in disasters, particularly cyclones, which have destroyed homes, businesses, marketplaces, crops, and infrastructure (ADB 2018). Pacific island countries are among the most vulnerable to the effects of climate change, including the risk of partial or total inundation following sea-level rise, due to their low elevation and small size (IPCC 2021). Impacts on women can be greater as their employment is often more vulnerable. There is a societal expectation that women are responsible for care work. Women are often not involved in decision-making regarding disaster risk reduction and climate change. Early warning systems do not always consider how to convey information to women. Women often lack land rights and access to productive assets that would support resilience, as well as social protection schemes designed to support recovery (FAO and SPC 2019; FAO 2019; UN Women 2016).

Considering gender equality in action on climate change and disaster risk reduction can create opportunities for women's economic empowerment. In Fiji, ADB worked with Habitat for Humanity Fiji to provide women with carpentry skills to support decisions around shelter preparedness in their communities and access employment opportunities in a historically male-dominated construction industry (ADB 2021).

Climate change is also affecting key industries that women rely on, such as agriculture, fisheries, and tourism due to increased extreme weather events, changes in precipitation, and sea-level rises (ADB 2019). Women agricultural workers in Papua New Guinea have reported an increased burden of work due to reduced soil fertility and erosion, and reduced yields, which also contributes to reduced income and food insecurity (Mcleoda et al. 2018). Following Cyclone Winston in 2016, mud crab fishers in Fiji, who are predominantly female, changed their fishing patterns; 52% stopped harvesting crabs as they needed to divert labor to repairing their homes and faced difficulties accessing collection sites and markets (Thomas et al. 2018). ILO (2017a) found that agricultural workers in the Pacific are unlikely to have skills in other income-generating activities, thus the effects of climate change are likely to push workers in remote areas into unemployment.

The effects of climate change are likely to increase migration flows, increasing the importance of considering the gendered experience of migration and entry into foreign labor markets (Oakes et al. 2016).

There is a lack of data on women entrepreneurs in green businesses. ADB, the ILO, and other development partners have warned that unless there are proactive efforts to include women in science, technology, engineering and mathematics (STEM) training, women will be excluded from the opportunities that emerge in the green economy (Asia Foundation 2021).

Women are organizing adaptation activities in their communities, such as introducing salt-tolerant crop varieties following flooding and saltwater intrusion (Mcleoda et al. 2018). For example, there is some evidence available on the roles women play in community organizing and leadership, and efforts to replant mangroves (Government of Samoa 2020).

How does access to digital technologies affect women's economic empowerment in the Pacific island countries?

The Pacific island region has the lowest rate of mobile internet penetration in the world at 18% and there is a gender gap in access (GSMA 2019). This has increased over recent years. In Samoa, mobile internet penetration increased from 41% of the population in 2013 to 88% in 2018; however, the proportion of private homes with access to mobile phones is higher among households headed by men than households headed by women (Government of Samoa 2020; UNFPA Pacific 2020). Multiple studies found that mobile phone usage reflects existing patterns of inequality and social norms. In matrilineal East New Britain, Papua New Guinea, women market sellers showed higher levels of phone usage than men, while in the patrilineal Western Highlands Province, the opposite trend was found (Curry et al. 2016).

Women have reported many benefits of digital technology for their businesses, including reaching new markets, reducing travel costs, using calculators, and ordering supplies (GSMA 2014). Women in Tonga have used Facebook to reach new markets, selling handicrafts to women in the diaspora (FAO and SPC 2019). Despite this, women may have lower awareness of the potential benefits of digital technology for their business. In Papua New Guinea, firms with majority-female ownership were less likely than men to view technology, including internet access, as an option to improve their business, favoring instead marketing and advertising services (Mishra et al. 2017).

Digital technology offers opportunities to improve access to financial services and promote the formalization and expansion of small businesses. Business owners can provide records of savings and transactions, which improves their ability to secure loans (UNESCAP 2020b). Despite this, there is a low uptake. In Samoa, where phone ownership is high, access to mobile banking is limited; only 3.7% of mobile phone owners had a mobile money account in 2015 (ADB 2018 cited in UNESCAP 2020a). During the COVID-19 pandemic, concerns were raised that lack of access to mobile money transfers would prevent access to community-based savings clubs (CARE 2020).

Barriers to accessing digital technology include price and the risk of violence and/or abuse. A survey of 509 women from low-income households in Papua New Guinea found that 96% of respondents said the cost of phone handsets and credit was too high, and 22% of women with a mobile phone said that it made their husbands suspicious (GSMA 2014). A study in Fiji found that cost was the strongest deterrent to using digital financial services, with 50% of participants agreeing or strongly agreeing that it was costly even though it generally costs less than sending a money order through the post office (Finau et al. 2016).

After a financial literacy training conducted by banks, only 27% of participants perceived digital financial services as costly. While women often have less access to common communication systems such as radio and text messaging, male household heads have more control over access to information as they are more likely to have access to the systems or to go to town to access information (CARE Australia 2020). This can act as a significant constraint to women's knowledge of, or engagement in training, employment, and other economic opportunities, including digital skills training (Asia Foundation 2021).

Industry in the Pacific island countries is becoming increasingly automated and digitalized (Asia Foundation 2021). Automation puts pressure on women's labor force participation, which often involves lower-skilled jobs, such as assembly line manufacturing, garment industry work, and food preparation and packaging. Women are overrepresented in these jobs, which are being automated (Asia Foundation 2021). Without access to digital skills training, women are at risk of being left behind.

Access to technology can improve the enabling environment for women's economic empowerment. For example, mWomen, a nonprofit initiative that began as a collaboration between Vodafone and the Ministry of Women, Children and Poverty Alleviation, offers free advice on legal rights relating to gender-based violence (GBV) via short messaging service (SMS) in Fiji (UN ESCAP 2016). In 2016, there were over 25,600 subscribers to the mWomen e-service, 65% of whom are women. Increased use of mobile phones and better boats have increased the number of women who go night fishing with their husbands in Kosrae and Yap States, Federated States of Micronesia, as it is now considered safer (Pacific Community 2019). Furthermore, in a 2014 survey of women in Papua New Guinea, 85% of mobile phone users reported an increased sense of independence (GSMA, 2014). There is an evidence gap on female digital entrepreneurs, for example, in FemTech or EdTech, in the Pacific island countries.

What progress have development partners and governments made toward increasing women's access to employment and control over income, and what are the current gaps?

In 2012, Pacific island leaders signed a Gender Equality Declaration, which explicitly includes women's economic empowerment and support for women in the formal and informal sectors (McKinnon et al. 2016; Pacific Community 2017). Finance ministers also adopted a Forum Economic Ministers' Meeting (FEMM) Action Plan in 2012, which includes specific priorities for women's economic empowerment (Pacific Community 2017), including increasing women's access to finance, business ownership, and markets; improving women's right to safe, fair, and equal participation in local economies; and improving access to and use of sex-disaggregated data (SPC 2014). This acknowledgment of the importance of the informal sector is significant, given women's concentration in this area and the limited opportunities in the formal sector.

Despite this, gaps in legislation persist as a barrier to women's economic empowerment, and there is some evidence that policies can reinforce stereotypes. A 2021 study found that where policy instruments in the Fijian fisheries sector discussed gender, they predominantly focused on women rather than considering gender roles or dynamics (Lawless et al. 2021). Furthermore, women were portrayed as vulnerable or victims in 35 out of 55 small-scale fisheries policy instruments, showing a paternalistic approach and a gap in understanding the benefits of women's participation and leadership in the fisheries sector.

Governments are also constrained by limited capacity, resources, and accountability for mainstreaming gender equality and women's economic empowerment. In the Cook Islands, the Australian Department of Foreign Affairs and Trade (DFAT 2019) identified a lack of capacity in the Gender Development Office, which had only two staff, and insufficient human and financial resources to mainstream gender and women's empowerment. In addition, there was limited production and use of sex-disaggregated data or gender analysis to inform policy making, program design, and service delivery.

Governments are taking steps to improve women's access to finance. The Denarau Action Plan on Gender and Women's Financial Inclusion was adopted by all the Pacific central banks and associated Alliance for Financial Inclusion members (AFI) in 2016. The plan calls for incorporating gender considerations in the AFI's network core activities, encouraging AFI members to set specific financial inclusion objectives and targets for women's financial inclusion, and collaborating and coordinating with key stakeholders in taking concrete steps to better understand the women's market segment (AFI 2016 cited in Pacific Women Shaping Pacific Development 2017). Other initiatives include a cottage industries program run by the Ministry of Agriculture in Fiji, which provides funds to women or women's groups for starting small market gardens, poultry projects, or other agricultural activities (FAO and SPC 2019). Box 2 presents an example of a project for increasing local government accountability to meet the needs of women market traders.

> ### Box 2: Increasing Local Government Accountability to Women Market Traders
>
> Through the Markets for Change (M4C) project, local government and councils in Fiji, Solomon Islands, and Vanuatu held regular consultations with Market Vendors Associations (MVAs) to discuss infrastructure improvements, budgets, and development of by-laws and ordinances. The project worked to strengthen accountability and capacity of market management and local governments in laying the groundwork for gender-responsive policies, procedures, and decision-making processes that would meet the needs of market vendors, especially women. The MVAs are predominantly made up of, and led by, women: 70% of the 7,500 members in 2015 were women, and 13 of 19 MVAs had over 50% women in leadership positions.
>
> Source: UN Women (2015).

Development partners are mainstreaming gender and implementing targeted projects. The Government of Australia is one of the largest development partners in the Pacific. Through its bilateral aid program and support to multilateral organizations such as the World Bank and ADB, it has taken a two-pronged approach of (i) encouraging mainstreaming of gender and women's empowerment across development-partner-funded projects, and (ii) providing targeted funding for projects and analytical work that aim to reduce gender gaps and empower women. Using grant funding and concessional loans, the World Bank and ADB are increasing the focus on gender across their programs including, among others, projects funding water supply and sanitation, agriculture, information and communication technology (ICT), transport, and private sector development. The DFAT-funded Pacific Women Shaping Pacific Development has been one of the largest investments in women's empowerment in the region. ADB's Pacific Private Sector Development Initiative (PPSDI) promotes women's economic empowerment with a focus on supporting women entrepreneurs and increasing women's participation in paid employment. IFC has worked with the private sector to promote women's leadership and improve gender equality in the workplace. Several pieces of relevant analytical work have been undertaken including a study on trade facilitation challenges for women traders by the World Bank (2021a), and on the impact of gender-based violence on business and productivity by IFC (2021).

Development partners have played a key role in ensuring interventions consider gender equality and women's economic empowerment. Increasingly, development partners have required that gender is considered at the planning, implementation, and monitoring stages of projects. Lambeth et al. (2014) found that this, along with increased awareness of the role women play in fisheries, leads to greater support for their activities. For example, courses that were previously only open to men now actively encourage women's participation.

Governments and development partners have organized a range of activities to promote women's economic empowerment. This includes awareness raising and training activities, such as national women and forest workshops held in Fiji (Secretariat of the Pacific Community 2014).

A number of governments have policies and skills programs to prepare workers for overseas employment, including in care, hospitality, tourism, and construction (Asia Foundation 2021).

Private sector organizations have also worked to increase women's access to employment. This includes gender-responsive policies at SolTuna in Solomon Islands, which offers maternity leave, access to accommodation, medical services, and GBV counseling (Keen and Hanich 2015). Mastercard, the Government of Australia, Fintech Pacific, and ygap (an international nongovernment organization) are collaborating to develop an easy-to-use, accessible payment acceptance platform for women-led small businesses in Fiji (Mastercard 2021). This platform would allow market stall vendors to accept payments on their mobile phones, enabling the MSMEs to increase revenue, strengthen their financial and digital literacy, and attract international visitors who often prefer to use digital payments.

A number of regional organizations are working to further women's economic empowerment, such as the Secretariat of the Pacific Community (SPC) and the Pacific Islands Forum Secretariat (PIFS). All Pacific island countries and territories, as well as Australia, France, New Zealand, and the United States are members of the SPC, which works to contribute to the development goals of its members.[16] SPC has worked to increase the participation of women in coastal fisheries, including by supporting women so they could assist with the development of community fisheries management plans and actively participate in Fisheries Management Committees, which used to be male-dominated (SPC 2014). The Pacific Islands Forum has 18 members.[17] It works to foster cooperation between governments and collaboration among international agencies, as well as to represent the interests of its members. It has organized regional learning forums on women's economic empowerment, and convenes Forum Economic Ministers Meetings where annual progress reports on women's economic empowerment are presented (PIFS 2020).

Ownership, Formalization, and Expansion of Businesses

Why do women work in the informal economy, and where are they positioned in the informal economy hierarchy?

There is strong evidence that in the Pacific, it is mainly women who work in the informal economy. This is particularly true of women in remote areas. Women tend to work in subsistence agriculture and fishing and as market vendors; some of them make garments and handicrafts. These are considered as low productivity jobs with limited start-up capital required and limited skill accumulation potential (ILO 2014; ADB 2019; UNCTAD 2020). Even within sectors, occupational segregation of informal work exists, wherein women earn less income than men. For instance, in fishing, men target finfish (mainly tuna) for commercial purposes while women target invertebrates such as octopus, lobsters, snails, tube worms, sea cucumbers, sea urchins, clams, seaweed, and other shellfish mainly for home consumption (Secretariat of the Pacific Community 2014).[18] In Papua New Guinea, crops are cultivated separately by women and men, with women's crops earning half of men's (Pacific Women Shaping Pacific Development 2020).

Low levels of labor force participation and concentration in the informal economy limit women's access to social protection, especially during old age, reinforcing vulnerability and poverty. Women comprise the majority of the older population in the Pacific and are mostly widowed, therefore cannot rely on financial support from their spouse. Projections indicate that the proportion of women among the "oldest old" (80 years and over) will increase by two-thirds by 2050, with the feminization of aging more pronounced in the Cook Islands, Kiribati, and Tonga (UNFPA 2014). Many older women work in the informal economy, which restricts their access to social protection. For instance, the Fiji National Provident Fund Scheme, a pension scheme for old-age retirement, only has 1% coverage to informal workers of whom the majority are women (ADB 2017).

Women tend to work in the lower segments of the informal work hierarchy as homeworkers and unpaid family workers (ADB 2019; ILO 2019e cited in Asia Foundation 2021). For example, in Solomon Islands, outside of the capital Honiara, 80% of women working in the agriculture sector are unpaid subsistence agriculturalists

---

[16]   The following island countries and territories are members of the SPC: American Samoa, the Cook Islands, French Polynesia, Fiji, Kiribati, New Caledonia, Northern Marianna Islands, Palau, Papua New Guinea, the Pitcairn Islands, Tokelau, Tonga, Tuvalu, Nauru, Niue, the Marshall Islands, the Federated States of Micronesia, Wallis and Futuna, Solomon Islands, Vanuatu, and Samoa.

[17]   Australia, the Cook Islands, the Federated States of Micronesia, Fiji, French Polynesia, Kiribati, Nauru, New Caledonia, New Zealand, Niue, Palau, Papua New Guinea, the Marshall Islands, Samoa, Solomon Islands, Tonga, Tuvalu, and Vanuatu.

[18]   Finfish are bony fish with fins as opposed to shellfish.

(Pacific Islands Forum Secretariat 2020). Men tend to work more on their own or with one or few partners, whereas women are more likely to work in a business operated by someone else in their household (ADB 2019).

Informal work often gives Pacific women greater flexibility to juggle their multiple responsibilities.
Women spend more than three times as many hours on unpaid care work as men (Pacific Women Shaping Pacific Development 2020 cited in Asia Foundation 2021). In Fiji, 71% of women outside of the labor market cited "household work" as the primary reason for not participating in paid work (FBOS and ILO 2018 cited in Asia Foundation 2021). Regionally, there are indications that younger men are starting to share a greater burden of unpaid care work with their wives and female relatives, although in Fiji, progress is stagnating and even deteriorating (Walton 2012).

Women remain in the informal economy for social and economic reasons, such as lack of awareness of the formalization process; lack of convenient access to regulatory authorities in remote areas; difficulties in accessing opportunities and markets due to geographical remoteness and lack of infrastructure; avoiding the demands of family and community for money; and compliance costs associated with labor regulations, taxes, and license fees (ADB 2018; UNCTAD 2020a). Business formalization, such as the ability to enter into contracts and legal protections, has not been well-communicated to women. In rural areas, where people tend to work in collectives, the existing formal business structures may not suit women who are currently operating in the informal economy. In Papua New Guinea, IFC (2016) reports that low levels of education and literacy limit opportunities for formal work for women; while in Samoa, despite women having higher levels of education than men, they still predominate in the informal economy especially in the small-scale, home-based work in fish marketing, handicrafts, retail, and tourism sectors.

What are the status and trends of women's entrepreneurship and women-owned micro, small, and medium-sized enterprises (e.g., size of business, ownership structures)?

Women's entrepreneurship is common in the Pacific region, and significantly higher than in developing Asia; however female ownership remains most prevalent in family-run, smaller, and informal firms.
As shown in Table 4, Pacific firms with female participation in ownership are more likely to be small and medium compared to those with a majority-female ownership, which are more likely to be medium in size. The IFC MSME Finance Gap data shows that the percentage of micro firms that are women-owned is wide ranging from 9% in Fiji to 66.3% in Tonga, with most Pacific island countries having between 40% and 49% of micro-sized firms owned by women (IFC 2018b). As women's businesses are disproportionately represented within the informal and MSME sectors, they may suffer disadvantages in the context of public procurement requirements (PPSDI 2017).

Table 4: Women's Business Ownership by Firm Size
(%)

		Pacific	Developing Asia
Firms with female participation in ownership	Small	60.0	38.8
	Medium	59.8	38.8
	Large	50.8	40.3
Firms with majority-female ownership	Small	24.3	19.9
	Medium	38.8	16.9
	Large	23.2	13.6

Notes: Regional averages are computed by taking simple averages of country point estimates. For each economy, only the latest available year of survey data are used in this computation. Statistics do not include data from the Cook Islands, Kiribati, the Marshall Islands, Nauru, Palau, and Tuvalu as data is unavailable. Calculations are based on data from World Bank Enterprise Surveys.
Source: ADB (2019).

A total of 90.2% of Pacific women-owned MSMEs are in the informal sector, which is higher than the global average of 80.2% (Figure 8). In Samoa, almost all women-owned MSMEs are in the informal sector (97.4%). Regionally, women are typically concentrated in industries that experience intense competition and generate lower returns, such as in agriculture and in the services sector like retail, restaurants, hospitality and tourism, and handicrafts (ADB 2018 cited in ADB 2019).

Figure 8: Percentage of Women-Owned MSMEs in the Informal Sector

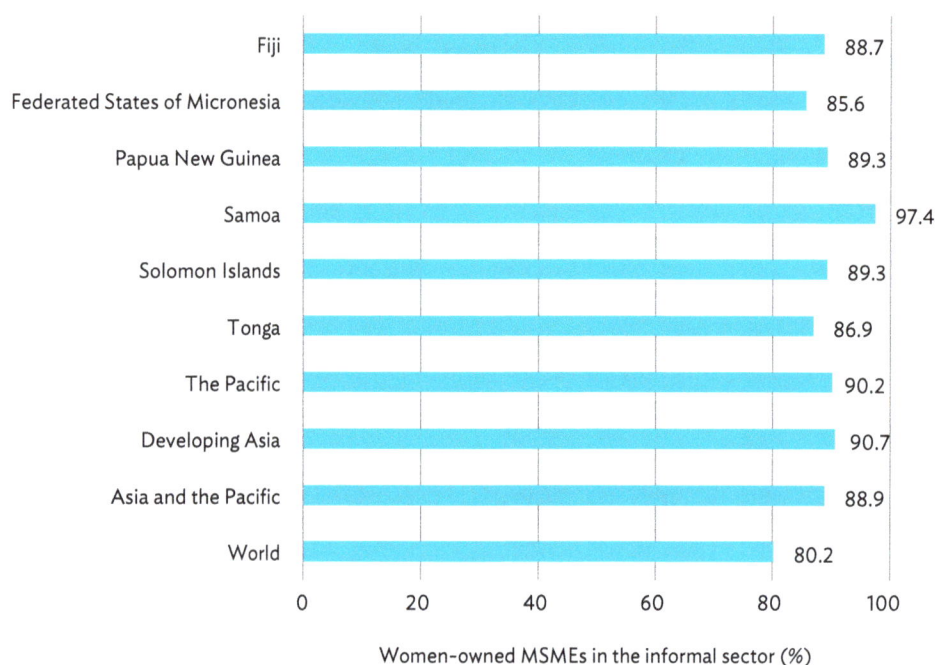

Region	%
Fiji	88.7
Federated States of Micronesia	85.6
Papua New Guinea	89.3
Samoa	97.4
Solomon Islands	89.3
Tonga	86.9
The Pacific	90.2
Developing Asia	90.7
Asia and the Pacific	88.9
World	80.2

Women-owned MSMEs in the informal sector (%)

MSMEs = micro, small, and medium-sized enterprises.
Note: Statistics do not include the Marshall Islands; Myanmar; Nauru; Palau; Taipei,China; Tuvalu; and Vanuatu.
Source: International Finance Corporation Enterprise Finance Gap Database (accessed April 2019) cited in ADB (2019).

There are 63.8% of firms with female participation in ownership in the Pacific services sector compared with 39.3% in developing Asia, and 32.6% of firms with a majority-female ownership in the Pacific services sector compared with 19.5% in developing Asia (ADB 2019). Statistics should be taken with caution, as they may disguise the fact that Pacific businesses are officially in men's names but are managed by women (Hedditch and Manuel 2010a; 2010b).

There is some evidence that women in the Pacific are increasingly setting up their own businesses and becoming entrepreneurs (Mohanty 2011; Narsey 2011 cited in Walton 2012; Government of the Cook Islands 2012; Lambeth et al. 2014; FAO 2019; UNESCAP 2020a). In Samoa, as agriculture moves toward being more market-driven, women in remote areas are seen to be the ones attending training to learn basic business skills (FAO 2019). Some women-owned businesses are becoming large enough that they can trade internationally. The Pacific Export Survey 2016 revealed that approximately 27% of exporting SMEs in the Pacific are run by women (UNESCAP 2020b).

Women-owned businesses in the Pacific—which mostly operate as micro, small, and medium-sized enterprises—tend to employ a higher proportion of women than large (mostly male-owned) firms (ADB 2019). In Papua New Guinea, SMEs with at least 50% female ownership have on average 58% of managers that are women, compared to SMEs with a majority male ownership that have 23% of managers that are women (Mishra et al. 2017).

How are women-owned micro, small, and medium-sized enterprises in the formal economy expanding?

There is limited evidence in the literature on how women-owned MSMEs in the formal economy are expanding. One route to expansion is to trade regionally or internationally, but there are generally fewer women-owned or -led businesses engaging in international markets compared with men-owned or -led businesses. An UNCTAD survey of 82 participants in Kiribati found that women in urban areas are more likely to formalize and expand their business using more sophisticated outlets, such as roadside stalls. They actively respond to emerging demand for various products and services. For example, in South Tarawa, women-owned businesses have met the growing demand for lunch meals from government offices and schools. In rural Kiribati in 2019, women handicraft producers attended government-organized training on handicraft design and skills. They also attended Women Expo in 2018 organized by the Ministry of Women, Youth and Sport to show their products, meet customers, and learn from each other (UNCTAD 2020).

What are the key barriers for women entrepreneurs and owners of micro, small, and medium-sized enterprises in the expansion and formalization of their businesses?

There is strong evidence on the wide-ranging set of barriers that women-owned MSMEs and women entrepreneurs experience in the expansion and formalization of their businesses:

Social norms. Culturally, in many contexts, women are not expected to become successful in business, which can act as a disincentive to expanding and formalizing a business. There is some regional variation, however, with growing acceptance of women's entrepreneurship in Tonga but a lack of entrepreneurial culture among women in Samoa and Fiji (IFC 2010; IFC 2016; Upadhyaya and Rosa 2019). In an ethnographic study of informal market vendors in Fiji, Upadhyaya, and Rosa (2019) found that both indigenous Fijian and Indo-Fijian women are repeatedly ridiculed for prioritizing economic gain and almost unanimously reveal that their families and friends look down on them. Similarly, in Samoa, women in remote areas do not usually receive community support for formal business development as it is perceived as diminishing their ability to fulfill family and social obligations (UNESCAP 2020b).

Often women have no option but to balance paid and unpaid care work responsibilities, which restrict their mobility and productivity and confine them to lower incomes. This is particularly true of women in remote areas, who tend to have greater responsibilities to engage in community activities than urban women (FAO 2019; UNCTAD 2020). However, in an UNCTAD survey, producers in remote areas were more likely to be confident in their own economic abilities, which translates into more initiative and less fear to expand their business, compared with their urban peers (UNCTAD 2020).

Social norms widely cited in the literature that harm women's ability to set up and sustain businesses are the concepts of *wantok* and *fa'alavelave*. *Wantok* means "one talk" and the concept is common to Papua New Guinea, Solomon Islands, and Vanuatu in Melanesia. It is an inbuilt social welfare practice within tribal and clan systems to ensure everyone's welfare, and may involve providing money and jobs to other tribal and/or clan members.

Wantok can also be a disincentive to savings and therefore a barrier to start and sustain a business. Women in Solomon Islands report that they are less likely than men to withstand pressure to help family members when called upon (Meleisea et al. 2015; ADB 2018a). A similar concept in Samoa is *fa'alavelave* ("an interruption"), which is a traditional ceremony where large amounts of money, food, and fine mats are accumulated, pooled, exchanged, and redistributed between kin-groups. Many women feel a disproportionate burden because these obligations require significant time and resources (Women's World Banking 2013 cited in UNESCAP 2020a). Women are also often not recognized for their contributions.

Access to commercial finance. Women-owned businesses experience greater barriers in accessing finance than men-owned businesses. IFC (2018a) finds that the aggregate finance gap of women-owned enterprises is sizable considering that, in general, most MSMEs are owned by men. In Fiji, microenterprises owned and operated by women ranked access to credit, access to insurance, and access to capital or savings (as well as access to market and logistical arrangements) as the top five challenges. Around 59% of respondents felt that if these challenges are addressed, medium to large growth in their business is possible (Sathye et al. 2018).

Fixed assets like land are important to securing collateral for commercial finance. Yet many women across the Pacific have limited access to land as they are excluded from traditional systems of land allotment (Hedditch and Manuel 2010b). Banks, therefore, are less likely to issue loans to women. Even if women-owned businesses can secure capital, social norms can influence slower or restricted business growth and/or diversified opportunities. For instance, in Samoa, women are more reluctant to go into debt and pay back loans as quickly as possible (UNESCAP 2020b). Using primary data from 25 interviews and 2 focus group discussions in Papua New Guinea, Nagarajan (2021) reported other barriers to accessing finance. These include a lack of financial expertise and experience, high equity requirements (20% to 50%), high interest rates (8% to 25% per annum), complex documentation requirements, fewer business networks, a lack of confidence, lower rates of mobile phone ownership, and poor digital literacy.

The legal foundations for secured transactions reform exist in a majority of Pacific Island countries. According to Holden and Pekmezovic (2019, 255) "As a group, the Pacific Island economies have been remarkable in the extent to which they have implemented secured transactions reforms." However, a detailed examination of the experiences in Solomon Islands and Vanuatu shows that intensive implementation support is still needed to increase the use and effectiveness of secured transactions as a foundation for lending (ADB 2014).

Business literacy, skills, and access to information. Studies from Fiji, Papua New Guinea, and Samoa suggest that many women have lower business literacy and skills than men, which can hamper expansion and formalization of business (Hedditch and Manuel 2010a; ADB 2015; IFC 2016; FAO 2019). Research undertaken by Pacific Private Sector Development Initiative in Papua New Guinea used focus groups and other approaches and found that women are 25% less financially literate than men (ADB 2015).

Research in Samoa by Hedditch and Manuel (2010a) found that women-owned businesses do not conduct a market analysis before starting a business and they are unable to prepare a business plan. In Kiribati, most women producers and traders from all age groups cited limited access to training and skills development programs as a major supply-side obstacle (UNCTAD 2020).

In addition to lower skills, women also have less access to timely and reliable market information. For example, women traders in Papua New Guinea and Samoa have more difficulty accessing information on border regulations and procedures than men (World Bank 2020a). In Papua New Guinea, women are less aware of relevant formalization requirements (PPSDI 2017). In Samoa, lack of awareness of compliance obligations is more prevalent in remote areas (Hedditch and Manuel 2010a).

Voice and accountability. Women in business are less likely to be regularly consulted for their views. For example, as shown in Figure 9, a survey of 1,260 traders in micro, small, medium-sized, and large firms in Fiji, Papua New Guinea, Samoa, and Vanuatu found that, except for Samoa, fewer women traders are consulted on any changes to official border processes and procedures than their men counterparts (World Bank 2020a). Women often have greater difficulty in accessing the justice system for resolving commercial disputes, have less confidence in dealing with institutions, and are less likely to complain (IFC 2010; ADB 2015; ADB 2018a). For instance, in a mixed-methods study in Fiji, women stated that they were afraid of raising issues to the council as they may not be allowed to sell their seafood products in the markets; and the council had not responded when previous complaints were made (Vitukawalu et al. 2020). This makes women more vulnerable to corrupt behavior from officials, which can act as a major barrier to earning income or sustaining a business (UNDP and UNODC 2020). Government officials tend to be more responsive to older and married women (Hedditch and Manuel 2010a).

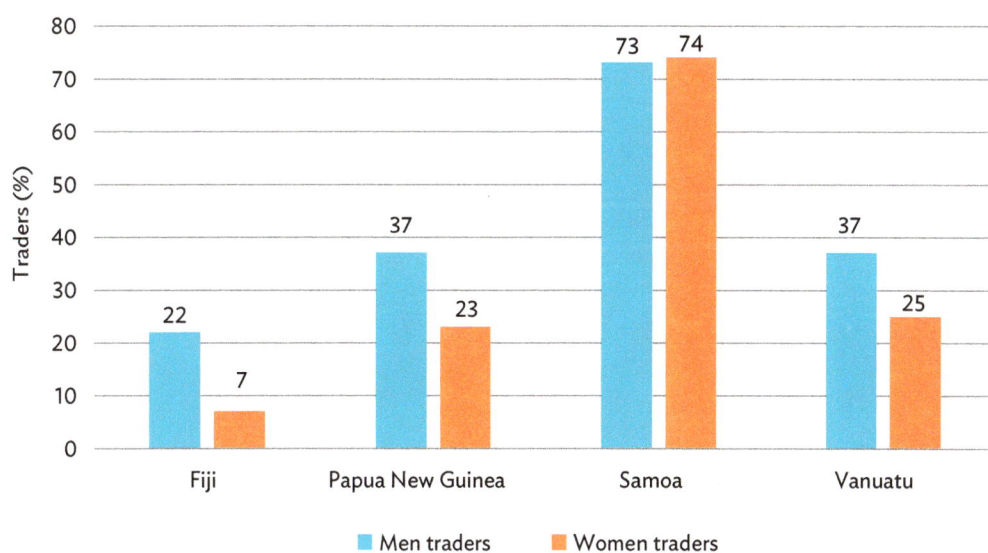

Figure 9: Percentage of Traders Who Are Regularly Consulted on Official Trade Processes and Procedures

Source: World Bank (2020a).

What is the status of social impact investing and gender lens investing? Who is providing capital for and investing into women-owned businesses? How has this changed?

Impact investment is nascent in the Pacific. The gender-lens investment that does occur is defined narrowly as investment in women-owned enterprises rather than, for example, including investments with impacts on women. DFAT-funded Pacific Readiness for Investment in Social Enterprise (Pacific RISE), designed to facilitate and grow the social impact investment market in the Pacific, took place from 2016 to 2021. However the program was influenced by traditional finance processes, resulting in a design that over-prioritized investor needs in relation to the needs of enterprises on the ground (Pacific RISE 2021). The pilot initiative found that the greatest demand for capital came from SMEs that were not able to access traditional forms of finance. Investing in these smaller businesses, however, was viewed as overly expensive and risky by many investors (Pacific RISE 2021).

There is weak evidence about how women entrepreneurs are using digital technologies to crowdfund and seek out peer-to-peer funding. Crowdfunding offers the double advantage of attracting more women investors within and outside the Pacific and providing more funding to women entrepreneurs in the region. Securing donations through crowdfunding is being utilized in Samoa, while peer-to-peer funding is being used in Papua New Guinea, although there is a lack of evidence of how these mechanisms have affected women-owned businesses in the region (ADB 2018). The Private Sector Development Initiative is supporting the set-up of national regulatory frameworks for crowdfunding and peer-to-peer lending in Papua New Guinea and Fiji, although work is at the early stage. These sources of innovative financing, which connected individuals across national borders using ICT, have a huge potential to benefit women-owned SMEs (ADB and Asia Foundation 2018). However, research from Latin America (Cincchiello and Kazemikhasragh 2021) and in equity crowdfunding campaigns run by technology ventures (Kleinert and Mochkabadi 2021) suggests that there are gender biases in investment decisions.

How does access to finance, digital technology, and other resources help women in business, including in business expansion?

Much of the literature focuses on the barriers that women face in accessing finance, digital technology, and other resources, rather than the opportunities that they provide. There is little information on what effect access to finance, digital technology, and other resources have had on women's businesses in the Pacific.

The evidence that does exist, however, is largely focused on the positive outcomes that women's access to finance can bring. Evidence from Solomon Islands shows that women's access to financial products correlates with a greater involvement in household spending and drives the establishment and growth of women-owned businesses (Pacific Financial Inclusion Program 2020). Pacific Women Shaping Pacific Development (2017) found that even though women are less likely to hold bank accounts in Fiji, Solomon Islands, and Vanuatu, those that have formal bank accounts are as likely (or more likely in Vanuatu) to report savings.

There are various initiatives that target the supply-side, demand-side, or both.

Supply-Side

Across the region, banks have expanded access to credit via a wider range of lending products, with more flexibility in eligibility criteria, lower rates of interest, and more flexible repayment schemes, which are more suited to women entrepreneurs (Pacific Islands Forum Secretariat 2021). The Private Sector Development Initiative has supported implementation of the secured transactions framework across the Pacific, which allows lenders to provide credit against the security of movable assets (PPSDI 2016 cited in Pacific Women Shaping Pacific Development 2017).[19] This is important as many women do not have land rights and therefore traditionally have not been able to use land as a collateral for financial services from financial institutions. Box 3 summarizes the progress of a secured transactions framework in Solomon Islands and Vanuatu, highlighting how the framework has enabled simplification and certainty because the framework has encouraged women to take out loans.

Although women have registered fewer security interests than have men, the simplified registry process and the certainty introduced by the new framework have encouraged women to take out loans. However, a lack of business skills and reluctance to approach lenders continue to be barriers (ADB 2014).

---

[19]   The Pacific Private Sector Development Initiative is a regional technical assistance program undertaken in partnership with the Government of Australia, the Government of New Zealand, and ADB. PPSDI works to reduce poverty and promote economic growth in the Pacific region through reforms that reduce the constraints to doing business and promote inclusive growth, entrepreneurship, and new business models.

Box 3: Secured Transaction Reforms in Solomon Islands and Vanuatu

In 2008, Solomon Islands and Vanuatu enacted secured transaction reforms. The reforms allowed the ability to assign movable property as collateral, rather than solely land or leases as loan security. Registry software was upgraded to gather data on borrowers' genders in 2010; but due to many security interests registered before that year, many have not recorded borrowers' genders. Nevertheless, women are actively using the secured transactions framework either as equal to men or as majority members.

	Gender of Borrowers with Secured Loan			
	Equally Men and Women	Majority Women	Majority Men	Indefinable
Solomon Islands	51	567	1,656	7,457
Vanuatu	166	222	919	1,719

Note: Data from June 2013.
Source: ADB (2014).

Recognizing that lending to women is profitable, development banks in the region also have focused on increasing lending to women, including women working in the informal economy.[20] For instance, in 2017, the Development Bank of Samoa issued 778 loans to women and youth with a total loan portfolio of $750,000 representing 1.3% of total lending. The majority of supported micro-sized enterprises were in the agriculture sector, but village shops and small-scale service businesses were also included (UNESCAP and UNCDF 2020).

Demand-Side

There is evidence of the importance of training and mentoring:

- The establishment of the Nauru Entrepreneurship Development Center (NEDC) in 2010, funded by the Government of Australia's aid program and implemented by the United Nations Development Programme (UNDP), provided a vehicle for SME advice, business training, mentoring, and microfinance support. The NEDC funded 14 business projects led by women, including 10 led by young women (ILO 2015).

- In Samoa, the provision of financial literacy and training from the central bank in partnership with the Development Bank of Samoa has helped unemployed women and survivors of domestic violence to establish 138 micro-businesses (ILO 2015).

- The Pacific Financial Inclusion Program has worked with service providers in (i) highlighting the importance and benefits of gender equality, (ii) designing the appropriate messaging to attract women as clients, and (iii) providing gender-sensitive financial education and mobile phone literacy training to clients.[21] This has built women's confidence and empowered them to make informed decisions about their business from budgeting, expenditure, to business management (Pacific Islands Forum Secretariat 2020).

[20] There has been little appetite from the major commercial banks in the Pacific to consider women as a viable market segment despite acknowledging that women are less likely to default on loan payments.
[21] The Pacific Financial Inclusion program ran from 2008 to 2020 and was jointly administered by the United Nations Capital Development Fund and the United Nations Development Programme. Operating in Fiji, Papua New Guinea, Samoa, Solomon Islands, Timor-Leste, Tonga, and Vanuatu, it received funding from the Government of Australia, the European Union, and the Government of New Zealand. The objective was to increase the number of low-income Pacific islanders who adopted formal financial services.

Supply- and Demand-Side

- South Pacific Business Development (SPBD) is a microfinance network in the Pacific that provides micro loans in Samoa from $470 to $3,000 to all its women clients. Prior to being granted loans, new recruits are trained on the loan program—wherein a savings account is created—as well as on financial literacy. The spouses of women borrowers can also join the training. SPBD has supported over 300 women clients to move from microfinance loans to small and medium-sized loans. However, the transition from micro to small and medium-sized loans has remained slow among women participants, with many of them remaining in the informal economy (ADB 2018 cited in UNESCAP 2020a).

Less information was found on access to digital technology. Women in the Pacific are less likely to have access to a computer or a smartphone, and the digital literacy skills to use online platforms. Yet evidence points that once women have gained access to ICT tools and services, they tend to use them equally as or more than men. When digitally connected, firm-level data shows that women-owned businesses are more likely to use emails to interact with clients (ADB 2019). Results from the 2017 Pacific Exporters Survey show that Pacific firms with women owners are more active online, with their own website and social media as the most popular channels (ADB 2019).

How has the legal and regulatory environment changed to be more responsive to women-owned micro, small, and medium-sized enterprises and women entrepreneurs? What lessons have been learned?

Many Pacific island countries have a weak enabling environment for promoting business and entrepreneurship, and constraints are felt disproportionately by women. When comparing Women, Business and the Law (WBL) entrepreneurship indicator scores from 2010 to 2021, the only difference is that the Marshall Islands now has laws that prohibit discrimination in access to credit based on gender. Other countries, except for Vanuatu, do not have this law (World Bank 2021d). In Vanuatu, small businesses pay the same percentage of tax as larger companies and global corporations, which has a regressive effect that impacts adversely on women who are concentrated in MSMEs (ADB 2018).

There have been several changes in the enabling environment, which have benefited women-owned micro, small, and medium-sized enterprises and women entrepreneurs. Digital processes are the most widely cited positive change on women-owned MSMEs and women entrepreneurs. For example, in Tonga, one can apply for a business license via traditional paper-based forms or through an online system. Applying online avoids transport costs and fees, which are particularly burdensome for time-poor women, although it does rely on an internet connection (IFC 2010; Pacific Women Shaping Pacific Development 2017). The online systems collect sex-disaggregated data that can provide governments with the information to improve systems and policies. In Fiji, the government has deployed staff to distribute forms and collect fees (Nagarajan 2016 cited in Pacific Women Shaping Pacific Development 2017a). Samoa, Papua New Guinea, and Fiji have adopted the following changes:

- **Samoa.** The Government of Samoa has attempted to shape the interpretation of *fa'alavelave* through recommending that families should limit the number of mats gifted at special occasions (ADB 2018). The Companies Act of 2008 ensured that a single shareholder can be registered, wherein a woman can start up a formal business registered as a company on her own without bringing a male relative as a second shareholder (Hedditch and Manuel 2010a).

- **Papua New Guinea.** The practice of women maintaining two bank accounts to enable them to keep business monies separate is supported by the country's financial institutions (ADB 2018).

- **Fiji.** To increase access to finance during the COVID-19 pandemic, the government has guaranteed to pay 75% of the principal outstanding on defaulted loans up to a limit of $75,000 per business on all micro, small, and medium-sized business loans to women entrepreneurs (Dahal and Wagle 2020).

There is emerging evidence of the potential benefit of gender-responsive procurement but few Pacific island countries have policy or legislative frameworks that explicitly support or actively promote it. Through gender-responsive public procurement policies and practices, governments and public buyers can promote gender equality and encourage suppliers to improve their performance on women's empowerment (OECD 2021). In 2021, Guam adopted a procurement policy in favor of women-owned businesses through the "The Support for Women-owned Businesses Act;" but it is too soon to determine the impact of this new policy on women's entrepreneurship in the country.

To what extent are women entrepreneurs and women-owned micro, small, and medium-sized enterprises organizing and networking more to shift the enabling environment?

There are a wide variety of business networks in the Pacific, but due to capacity and funding gaps their remit is mainly around building assets, capabilities, and opportunities for women. There is little evidence of seeking transformational change that address unequal power relations and systemic institutional, legal, and societal changes.[22] Pacific Women Shaping Pacific Development (2017) notes that the status of collective action, organization, and leadership around women's economic empowerment in the Pacific is relatively underdeveloped compared to other women's rights movements, especially in political leadership and ending GBV. National-level business networks representing the interests and concerns of businesswomen in the Pacific are present in the Cook Islands, Fiji, the Marshall Islands, Papua New Guinea, Samoa, and Solomon Islands (Table 5). However, it is not clear whether there have been increases in networking recently, except for the Women Entrepreneur Network in the Marshall Islands which was revived in 2020. New Zealand and Australia are the main development partners across business networks in the Pacific.

Table 5: National Business Networks in the Pacific Targeting Women

Name of Business Network	Date of Establishment and Development Partner Support	Country	Purpose
Women in Business Association	2004, DFAT	Solomon Islands	Promote and build business opportunities for women to participate at all levels, focusing on helping women overcome the barriers to business.
Business Coalition for Women	2012, DFAT's Pacific Women Shaping Pacific Development	Papua New Guinea	Provide training and advisory services across four main pillars: (i) eliminating violence against women, (ii) promoting women to leadership roles, (iii) recruitment and retention of women, and (iv) opportunities for women in supply chains.
Women in Business Development	1991, New Zealand Aid Development, Oxfam New Zealand, Canada Fund	Samoa	Provide capacity building support for businesses that honor indigenous traditions; assist businesswomen in identifying and gaining access to markets; and promote disaster preparedness and food security among members.

continued on next page

[22] Examples of transformational change are promoting and advocating on protective legal, regulatory, and policy frameworks; challenging social norms; tackling discriminatory attitudes; amplifying women's collective voice and action; supporting women to negotiate and participate in innovative benefit-sharing schemes, such as land titles for women; establishing social accountability mechanisms for quality service delivery; and recognizing, redistributing, and reducing household/caring responsibilities. See Caroline Moser's Gender and Inclusion Framework (2016) cited in Prosperity Fund (unpublished).

Table 5 *continued*

Name of Business Network	Date of Establishment and Development Partner Support	Country	Purpose
Samoa Business Hub (SBH) (formerly known as Small Business Enterprise Center)	1994, Government of Samoa, New Zealand Ministry of Foreign Affairs and Trade (MFAT)	Samoa	Provide services and advice to grow MSMEs into large businesses. More than 50% of MSMEs that SBH supports are women-owned or -managed. (UNESCAP 2020b).
Women Entrepreneur Network	Revived in 2020, unclear	Marshall Islands	Recent activities include business continuity planning related to COVID-19 and determining how the network will be developed and what training is needed. (Currently no website.)
Business and Professional Women (CIBPW)	Unclear	Cook Islands	Develop skills in business leadership.
Women Entrepreneurs and Business Council (WEBC)	2013, unclear	Fiji	Advocate for and support women entrepreneurs in Fiji. WEBC is affiliated with the Fiji Commerce and Employers Federation.

COVID-19 = coronavirus disease, DFAT = Department of Foreign Affairs and Trade of Australia, MSMEs = micro, small, and medium-sized enterprises.

Note: Groups that fully target or significantly target women are included. There is a Facebook group called "Women Entrepreneurs Network of Samoa" but the last post was in 2015 and it is unclear whether the group is still operational.

Source: Social Development Direct.

The Pacific Islands Private Sector Organization (PIPSO), a representative body at the regional level, advocates on behalf of business, including women in business in the region.[23] With small budgets, little capacity, and few staff, these networks provide business and financial training to women (ADB 2018). In some countries, Chambers of Commerce (or equivalent) offer a range of training programs targeted at women entrepreneurs (Pacific Islands Forum Secretariat 2021). In Fiji, the Women's Fund Fiji, a feminist grant mechanism, supports women's groups and networks through funding and capacity development, including advice on starting micro-businesses (Pacific Women Shaping Pacific Development 2021a).

Women in Business Development Inc. (WIBDI) in Samoa is the most well-established business network and has achieved considerable success through promoting and supporting organic certification of agricultural enterprises. It has helped in putting more than $200,000 in the hands of farmers annually through supplying well-known multinationals such as The Body Shop (Bafana and Hosenally 2019). WIBDI partnered with a Samoan technical services company Skyeye to map certified organic farms and has an accurate database of its production capacities (Defait 2018). It has also formed a marketing partnership with the café chain C1Expresso in New Zealand.

There are also networks at the local level where women are supporting each other in business. These include village women's committees and church groups, and in Kiribati, these small groups are increasingly consulted by Island Councils (UNCTAD 2020).

In Fiji, self-generated networks are being used to manage competition and innovate marketing strategies in the fishing industry (Michalena et al. 2020). There are also market vendor associations and union and/or employee associations. The UN Women Markets for Change Project in Fiji, Papua New Guinea, Solomon Islands, and Vanuatu has formed 12 market associations comprising 3,500 members. Women lead 9 out of 12 associations and hold 50%

---

[23] PIPSO http://www.pipso.org.fj/ has a subbranch known as Pacific Women in Business. For this group, there is only a Facebook page but this was last updated in 2016.

of the leadership positions (Pacific Islands Forum Secretariat 2020). These associations have made improvements in market facilities and security (Pacific Islands Forum Secretariat 2020). In Fiji, there is some evidence of patronage and identity-based politics within local-level groups (Vilisoni 2018; Upadhyaya and Rose 2019).

Association Between Women's Economic Empowerment and Violence Against Women and Girls

What are the intersections between women's economic empowerment and violence against women and girls in Pacific island countries, for women-owned micro, small, and medium-sized enterprises and women entrepreneurs?

Rates of violence against women and girls across the Pacific region are some of the highest in the world, though they differ widely among countries, and marginalized communities are likely to face even higher rates of violence. As shown in Figure 10, in Fiji, Kiribati, the Marshall Islands, Papua New Guinea, Solomon Islands, and Vanuatu, 50% or more women have been subjected to physical and/or sexual violence by an intimate partner in their lifetime, compared to the global average of 30%. The only Pacific country with a rate below the global average is Palau at 25% (WHO 2018). There is no comparable data available for Niue, as no population surveys on intimate partner violence have been carried out (Thomas 2017). There is little data available on marginalized communities, but evidence has shown 84% of lesbians, bisexual, and transgender masculine and gender nonconforming people in Fiji have experienced intimate partner violence (DIVA for Equality 2019). Rural women are more likely than urban women (69% versus 58%) to experience violence during their lifetime in Fiji (FWCC 2013). According to the Samoan 2017 Family Safety Study, 90% of elderly men and women interviewed in Samoa suffered emotional or physical abuse; while all people with disabilities interviewed experienced multiple forms of violence (Government of Samoa Ministry of Women, Community and Social Development 2018).

Figure 10: Women Who Experience Partner Violence in Pacific Island Countries

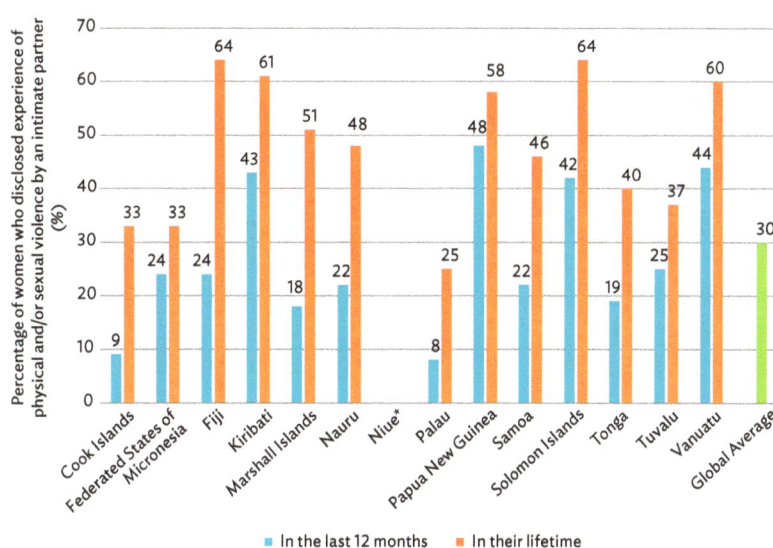

* No data is available for Niue.
Source: UNFPA (2020).

Economic abuse is prevalent in the Pacific region, negatively impacting women's economic empowerment by impeding their control over economic assets. In the Marshall Islands, 27% of ever-partnered women reported that their partners either took their earnings or refused to give them money (ADB 2019). In Fiji, 28% of ever-partnered women have partners who either take their savings or refuse to give them money, with rural women experiencing this economic abuse at higher rates (33%) than urban women (24%) (FWCC 2013). In Solomon Islands, 19% of those who have experienced intimate partner violence have also had their earnings or savings taken from them by their partner (SPC 2009). Not having control of one's own income directly impedes women's economic empowerment and ability to make business decisions. No evidence was found on the specific impacts of economic abuse for women-owned MSMEs and women entrepreneurs in the Pacific.

Reproductive coercion is also prevalent in the Pacific region, limiting women's economic empowerment by impeding their voice and agency. A Family Health and Safety survey in Solomon Islands found that 11.6% of currently partnered women in each country who had experienced physical or sexual partner violence reported they had experienced a partner trying to stop family planning (SPC 2009). In a study of respondents in Fiji who have experienced physical and/or sexual partner violence, 10.2% reported that their partner had refused or stopped contraception, and 13.6% stated that their current or most recent partner refused to use a condom (FWCC 2013). In Vanuatu, a needs assessment identified that 14% to 21% of women wishing to use family planning methods and 74% to 78% of women wanting to use condoms have either been subjected to or fearful of physical and sexual violence from their intimate partner (UNFPA 2015). This type of reproductive coercion is a form of violence against women and girls, and negatively impacts women's economic empowerment when it leads to girls dropping out of school due to early marriage and pregnancy and when it results in increased unpaid care work. It also limits women's access to economic opportunities leading to a concentration of women in informal work (CARE Australia and UNFPA 2020). No evidence was found on what the specific impacts of reproductive coercion are for women-owned MSMEs and women entrepreneurs in the Pacific.

There is some evidence that women's increasing income is correlated with increased intimate partner violence. However, few studies have addressed the relationship between women's economic empowerment and VAWG in the Pacific specifically for women-owned MSMEs and women entrepreneurs. Research in Solomon Islands and Papua New Guinea, which included 485 interviews, found that men use intimate partner violence to reassert their power over women enrolled in economic empowerment programs (Eves et al. 2018). Qualitative research by Women's World Banking on women's financial inclusion in Papua New Guinea and Samoa found strong links between money, household conflict, and domestic violence. The report recommends offering safe, confidential financial services for women to protect their money and assets (Banthia et al. 2013). In Vanuatu, women who have their own source of income are around 150% more likely to experience physical and sexual violence than those who do not (ADB 2019). Making decisions about household finances in general is a major reason for family tension and violence in the Pacific region (Chattier 2014; Meleisea et al. 2015; Eves et al. 2018). While the rationale for women's economic empowerment is strong, interventions need to be designed carefully to mitigate the risk of increased intimate partner violence.

Increased economic empowerment can also be an enabler for women to leave a violent relationship. The relationship between women's economic empowerment and violence against women and girls is bidirectional. In the Pacific region, economic dependence on a husband is a major barrier to women from leaving a violent relationship (AusAID ODE 2008). In Fiji, a survey of 3,538 households found a complex relationship—on the one hand, employment and women's economic empowerment can be a key pathway to support women to leave a violent relationship. On the other hand, partner violence can impact on women's income generation, with almost half (48%) of women who experience violence saying their work was disrupted in some way. Women with higher incomes than their husbands are also significantly more likely to experience partner violence, suggesting possible risks for women entrepreneurs (FWCC 2013).

Two recent assessments of the Fiji Women's Fund partners found that addressing the risks of violence against women and girls is important in interventions aimed at economically empowering women.
A 2019 impact assessment by Rise Beyond the Reef, a nongovernment organization focusing on rural and remote communities in Fiji, found no evidence of increased violence due to their sustainable income-generating projects. Men and women instead noted that increased earnings had lessened stress and tension in the household, with 98% reporting more amicable husband–wife relationships (Vunisea and Fleming 2019). This may be due to the program design, which recognized the ongoing risk of violence from the start. The program had the explicit objective of addressing gender inequities and domestic violence, conducted a baseline survey in the communities to assess changes over time, delivered GBV training, and created a community of "on-the-ground champions" as a long-term community development approach to address GBV and other harmful social norms (Fleming et al. 2020). The Spa Academy, which provides scholarships for a Certificate Level IV in Beauty and Spa Therapy for women from low socioeconomic backgrounds and from rural areas in Fiji, found no evidence of violence against women linked to the increased income of rural scholarship recipients (Fleming 2019).[24] This could be because scholarship recipients move away from their community to live at Spa Academy accommodation.

Women entrepreneurs face violence and harassment at work and on their way to and from work, which can restrict their income-generating activities. A study in Fiji found that 20% of women experienced sexual harassment at work in 2016, down from 33% in 2002 (Fiji Women's Rights Movement 2016). Marketplaces can be unsafe, specifically open markets in urban areas. Toilet facilities are often particularly unsafe, and women risk sexual harassment or assault when using them (Pacific Islands Forum Secretariat 2020). A study of fisherwomen in Fiji found that 59% of interviewees considered the market a safe place to sell their catch if they have a license; but women in focus groups reported that they were sometimes harassed and threatened while selling their catch (Thomas et al. 2021). For women selling at open urban markets in Papua New Guinea, insecurity is also a major concern (World Bank Group 2014). A UN Women (2011) scoping study of the markets in Port Moresby, Papua New Guinea, found that 55% of women and girl study participants reported experiencing some form of violence in the marketplace, while 22% of female market vendor respondents reported experiencing more than one incidence of sexual violence in the marketplace in the last 12 months. Security challenges such as these restrict women's mobility, excluding them from participating in income activities like selling produce to exporters or working as agribusiness extension agents (Government of Papua New Guinea National Statistics Office 2012; World Bank Group 2014).

When employees experience violence at home, there is a high cost to businesses. There is a relatively strong evidence base on this link in the Pacific. An IFC survey of 1,200 employees in Solomon Islands found that lost work time due to violence at home totals two working weeks per year per employee due to feeling distracted, tired, unwell, or being late or absent (IFC 2019c). A further week per employee per year is spent informally responding to the impacts of domestic and sexual violence in the workplace, such as through ad hoc conversations (IFC 2019c). In Fiji, a study of three companies found 10 workdays lost per employee, with 47% of all survey participants experiencing an impact on their work from domestic violence against themselves or a friend (IFC 2019c). In Papua New Guinea, IFC found that family and sexual violence translates to losing 10 days per employee per year, costing companies over $2.1 million per year. This cost was mainly due to feelings of anxiety, depression or shame, feeling drained, needing time off to attend court hearings, and feeling stressed because of the perpetrator's jealousy toward colleagues (IFC 2021). Similarly, a 2015 study in Papua New Guinea found that staff lost 11.1 days of work per year due to GBV, representing 2% of a firm's total salary bills and 9% of another's (Darko et al. 2015). Data for six countries shows that there is also a cost more generally on women's work, including women-owned MSMEs (Figure 11).

---

[24] Through the Fiji Women's Fund, part of the Pacific Women Shaping Pacific Development program, DFAT has been providing funding to the Spa Academy in Fiji. The funding provides scholarships for women from low socioeconomic backgrounds and from rural and remote areas where access to employment is low. Scholarships support these women to complete a Certificate Level IV in Beauty and Spa Therapy. Program funding covers costs for certificate level study over 8 months and the recipients are encouraged to save for the diploma level qualification, which is considered to give them a better footing for employment opportunities (Fleming 2019).

Figure 11: Impact of Partner Violence on Women's Paid Work

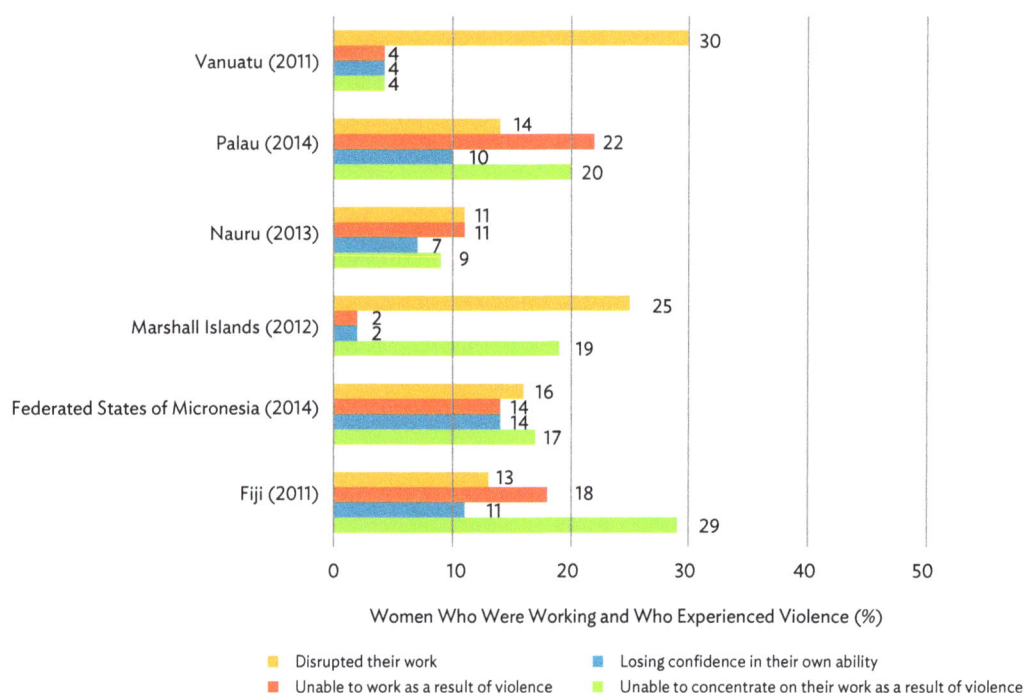

Vanuatu (2011)
- 30
- 4
- 4
- 4

Palau (2014)
- 14
- 22
- 10
- 20

Nauru (2013)
- 11
- 11
- 7
- 9

Marshall Islands (2012)
- 25
- 2
- 2
- 19

Federated States of Micronesia (2014)
- 16
- 14
- 14
- 17

Fiji (2011)
- 13
- 18
- 11
- 29

X-axis: 0, 10, 20, 30, 40, 50

Women Who Were Working and Who Experienced Violence (%)

Legend:
- Disrupted their work
- Losing confidence in their own ability
- Unable to work as a result of violence
- Unable to concentrate on their work as a result of violence

Source: Pacific Data Hub (2021b). For Vanuatu, data is from Vanuatu Women's Centre. 2011. *Vanuatu National Survey on Women's Lives and Family Relationships*. Port Vila, page 139.

What interventions by governments, development partners, civil society, or the private sector have addressed violence experienced by women entrepreneurs and women owners of micro, small, and medium-sized enterprises? What evidence is there on the effectiveness of these interventions on preventing and responding to violence?

There is an absence of comprehensive legislation on violence against women and girls, particularly sexual harassment, in the workplace across the Pacific region. Only Fiji, Kiribati, and Samoa have specific legislation on sexual harassment in the workplace (World Bank 2021d), while in other countries, the issue may be covered by criminal law or public service policies (ILO 2014). Only Fiji has ratified ILO Convention 190 (C190), an international treaty on violence and harassment at work (Center for Women's Global Leadership 2021). As of 2014, Tuvalu was the only Pacific country where a victim had successfully won a formal court case against her employer after being sexually harassed at work (ILO 2014).

There has been a successful intervention by civil society to improve legislation on violence against women and girls in the workplace. After a study in Fiji which found that 1 in 5 women had experienced sexual harassment in the workplace, the Fiji Women's Rights Movement initiated the "Not OK: Stop Sexual Harassment" campaign, which included publishing and disseminating infographic posters and resources on stopping sexual harassment. This campaign was part of a successful lobby to ratify C190, making Fiji one of only 25 countries in the world where the C190 ratification is in force (Center for Women's Global Leadership 2021).

Businesses and women's business networks often play a key role in awareness and support to address violence against women and girls in the Pacific region (ADB 2018). The Papua New Guinea Business Coalition for Women (BCW) is actively working with large companies to address violence against women and girls. They have recently published resources on the business costs of violence, developed culturally appropriate workplace policies and practices for companies, and provided training and support on the policies (Papua New Guinea BCW 2021). In Fiji, mWomen is a subscription-based SMS service giving free advice on women's legal rights on GBV. It began as a collaboration between Vodafone and the Department of Women (UNESCAP 2018). According to the Department of Women, in 2018, there were 25,613 subscribers (UNESCAP 2018).

The recently finished DFAT-funded Pacific Women Shaping Pacific Development (Pacific Women) program provides examples of effective interventions for addressing violence against women and girls for women workers and entrepreneurs. Pacific Women has addressed women's economic empowerment and violence against women and girls simultaneously, funding interventions such as community awareness and outreach activities (DFAT 2020). In partnership with the UN Women Safe Cities program, the Meri Seif (Woman Safe) subsidized a bus scheme in Port Moresby and Lae, Papua New Guinea, which runs exclusively for women and girls (UN Women 2019). The buses have provided an estimated 141,902 women and girls a safe journey to their job, school, or the market (Pacific Women Shaping Pacific Development 2021c). Further infrastructure improvements include safe accommodation centers and indoor toilet facilities for women vendors in Fiji and Papua New Guinea, which according to reports from women, have made them feel safer (Pacific Women Shaping Pacific Development 2021c).

Early signs show that interventions partnering with the private sector in the Pacific region are effective in addressing violence experienced by women workers. Fifteen large companies in Solomon Islands, covering 6,000 employees, have committed to introducing policies for respectful workplaces under the Waka Mere Commitment to Action (Pacific Women Shaping Pacific Development 2021c).[25] An IFC survey shows much lower levels of acceptance of violence among Waka Mere employees than previous studies, suggesting that the workplace responses have had a positive effect (IFC 2019c). The Bel isi project in Papua New Guinea delivered family and sexual violence awareness training to 3,961 employees across 15 companies (Pacific Women Shaping Pacific Development 2021c).[26] There are early signs that the Bel isi project is making a positive impact. Staff who experienced violence in the past 12 months were more likely to receive paid time off, counseling, and a referral to a relevant service than those who faced violence more than 12 months ago according to a survey (IFC 2021). Staff also reported that more positive things happened after disclosing to a trained staff member than disclosing to an untrained colleague (IFC 2021). No similar evidence was found for interventions targeting women entrepreneurs or women-owned MSMEs.

Development partners have increasingly focused on the unintended risks of violence against women and girls and sexual exploitation, abuse, and harassment from their projects, and put in place Do No Harm strategies. DFAT has adopted a prevention policy against sexual exploitation, abuse, and harassment (SEAH) and a "Do No Harm" toolkit, containing resources to support organizations at the community level working on women's economic empowerment projects for integrating approaches to address violence against women and girls into their project activities (IWDA 2018b). Similarly, the Inter-American Development Bank (IDB) and the World Bank have produced a resource guide and tools for their staff for integrating initiatives to address violence within their work (Global Women's Institute 2014). Since 2010, IDB has had extensive gender

---

[25]   The Waka Mere Commitment to Action is a 2-year initiative led by IFC in collaboration with Solomon Islands Chamber of Commerce and Industry (SICCI). Through Waka Mere ("She Works" in pidgin), 15 of the largest companies in Solomon Islands have committed to improve policies in one or more of the following three areas: (i) promote women in leadership, (ii) build respectful and supportive workplaces, and (iii) increase opportunities for women in jobs traditionally held by men (IFC 2018b).

[26]   The Bel isi project is a public–private partnership in Papua New Guinea, which aims to work with the private sector to play a transformational leadership role in changing attitudes toward family and sexual violence and improving services for survivors. There are 15 subscribing companies, and the supporting development partners include the DFAT-funded Pacific Women Shaping Pacific Development program, Business Coalition for Women, and the Government of Papua New Guinea (Bel isi Papua New Guinea 2021).

provisions, requiring borrowers to address gender-related risks including gender-based exclusion and sexual and gender-based violence (sexual exploitation, human trafficking) and the spread of sexually transmitted infections (IDB 2010). The Asian Infrastructure Investment Bank (AIIB) has recently updated its environmental and social framework, which includes explicit reference to preventing GBV and SEAH (AIIB 2021). ADB recently finalized a SEAH Good Practice Note which will be piloted in five countries, including one Pacific Island Country.

Effects of the COVID-19 Pandemic

How have women entrepreneurs and women-owned micro, small, and medium-sized enterprises been affected by the COVID-19 pandemic? How has the COVID-19 pandemic altered women's access to resources and opportunities as well as voice and agency?

The impacts of the COVID-19 pandemic on economic empowerment have been gendered. Despite low rates of COVID-19 across the Pacific region until the start of 2022, women have been negatively affected by government response measures such as lockdowns, school closures, and border closures. Women are more likely to work in the informal economy, where jobs are more precarious in the face of shocks due to a lack of contracts, and there is also a lack of paid sick leave if workers contract COVID-19. There have been large increases in the cost of food, which women in the Pacific are responsible for sourcing as well as preparing and cooking for families, and often sell in the food markets. Levels of unpaid care work, already high in the Pacific, have increased due to children being out of school, additional community disease prevention work, and unemployed relatives returning from urban areas or jobs abroad. These factors have led to women in the Pacific region being disproportionately impacted by the COVID-19 pandemic, reversing the key gains in women's economic empowerment over the past years (Pacific Women Shaping Pacific Development 2021b).

Women entrepreneurs, women-owned micro, small, and medium-sized enterprises, and women workers have been negatively affected by global travel restrictions. The tourism industry has been disproportionately affected due to global travel restrictions and accounts for up to 50% of economic activity in countries such as Fiji, Palau, Samoa, and Vanuatu (Center for Humanitarian Leadership 2020). In Fiji, tourism is particularly important for women-owned MSMEs selling to tourists; and as employees, women tend to work in part-time casual tourism-related jobs such as receptionists and cleaners (COVID-19 Response Gender WG 2020). International border closures have also affected women migrant workers, who have been unable to travel to seasonal work programs or have been unable to travel home and unable to qualify for government benefits (Howes 2020). Women migrant workers who are stranded abroad may face particular challenges in accessing safe accommodation and health care (Center for Humanitarian Leadership 2020).

There is strong evidence that the pandemic has affected women-owned micro, small, and medium-sized enterprises worse than male-owned businesses. The Pacific Trade Invest (PTI) Pacific Business Monitor surveys are providing critical regular data on how the COVID-19 pandemic is affecting businesses. As of July 2022, there had been 19 surveys since May 2020. PTI Pacific Business Monitor reports in July 2020 and December 2021 included a focus on women-owned businesses. As shown in Figure 12, in July 2020, 77% of women-owned businesses in the Pacific had experienced a significant decline in revenue to date, compared to 65% of male-owned businesses (PTI 2020). By November 2021, this had decreased to 69% of women-owned businesses and 39% of male-owned businesses.

Figure 12: Total Percentage of Pacific Female- and Male-Owned or Led Businesses Reporting a Decline in Revenue (July 2020)

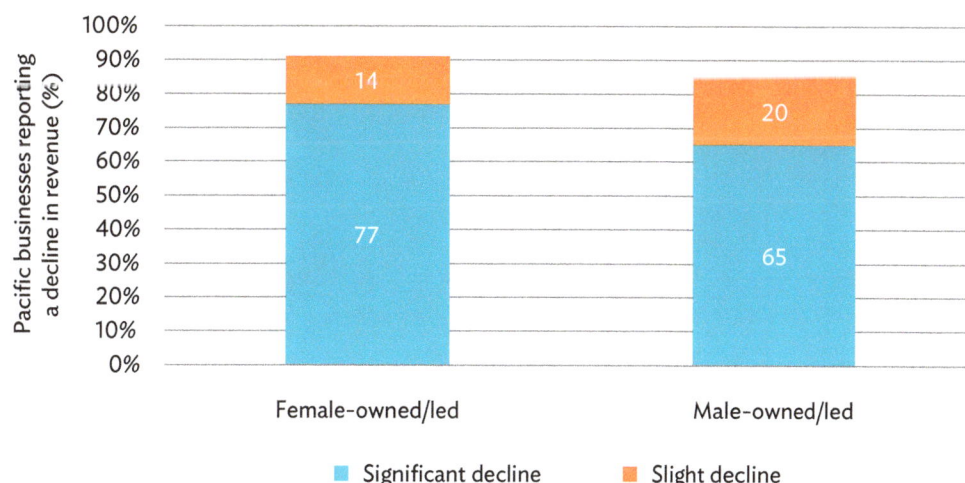

Notes: Pacific Trade Invest (PTI) (2020) is based on 134 businesses across the Pacific island countries that participated in the regular PTI Pacific Business Monitor surveys from 29 June 2020 to 12 July 2020, with 51% of businesses identifying as female-owned/led. PTI (2021) is based on eight surveys which took place from January 2021 to November 2021. Over 100 businesses participated in each survey, with between 43% and 53% identifying as female-owned/led businesses.
Sources: PTI (2020; 2021).

The 2020 survey found that 41% of female-owned businesses had temporarily closed compared to 29% of male-owned businesses (PTI 2020). By the end of 2021, 20% of female-owned businesses had temporarily closed compared to 8% of male-owned businesses (PTI 2021). The percentage of female-owned businesses that were permanently closed increased from July 2020 to November 2021 (2% to 3%) while the number of male-owned businesses that were permanently closed decreased (2% to 0%) (Figure 13). In both 2020 and 2021, both female-owned and male-owned businesses reported that their top three challenges were not knowing how long the crisis will last, poor cash flow, and the impact of closed international borders. However, female-owned businesses were 5% to 6% more likely to report these as somewhat or very challenging. In 2021, the biggest variance was in limited access to finance or capital and the increasing costs of products and raw materials. For both challenges, female-owned businesses were 12% more likely to report these as somewhat or very challenging.

There is some evidence suggesting that the most severely affected women-owned businesses are those that are newer and have more than five employees. In-depth annual surveys of women-owned MSMEs in Papua New Guinea found that 83.2% were negatively impacted by the COVID-19 pandemic while 26.8% reported temporary closure because of the pandemic. Women in start-up businesses are more likely to close than those that have already established businesses, although both faced significant challenges (CIPE 2020). Women with more than five employees felt the negative effects of COVID-19 more than those with fewer than five employees (CIPE 2021). This implies that women-owned microenterprises are faring better than SMEs, perhaps due to lower operational costs or because they work in sectors that have fared better. Higher education levels do not appear to be correlated with the impacts of the COVID-19 pandemic—67% of women entrepreneurs with a university degree experienced the negative effects of the pandemic (CIPE 2021). In Papua New Guinea, women entrepreneurs located outside of Port Moresby experienced a higher reduction in wages, compared to those in the capital (CIPE 2021).

Figure 13: Status of Pacific Businesses (July 2020, November 2021)

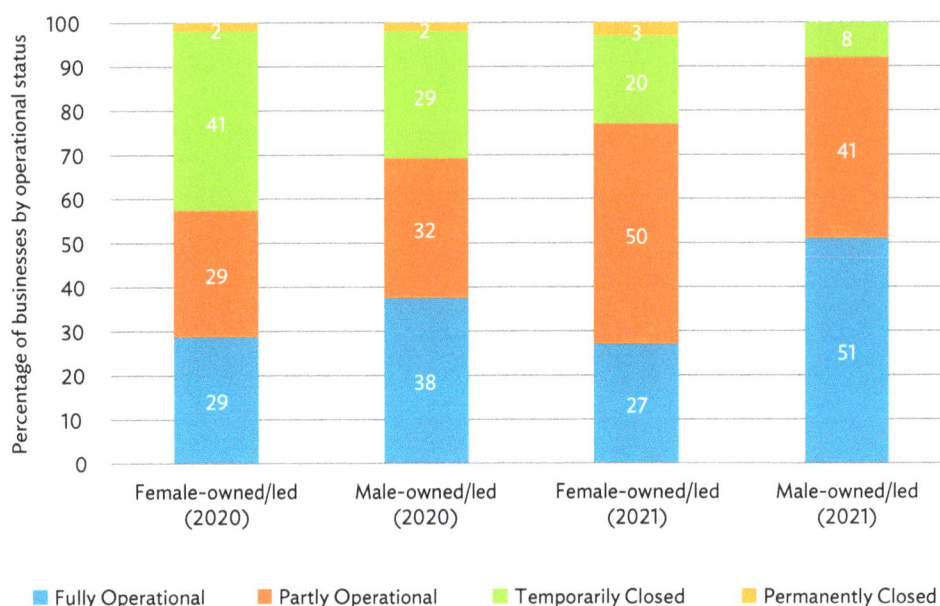

Sources: PTI (2020; 2021).

There is mixed evidence on the effects of the pandemic on women entrepreneurs and workers in the informal economy. A survey of 144 women entrepreneurs in Papua New Guinea found that COVID-19 had more negative effects on women's registered businesses compared to women with unregistered businesses. This could be because businesses in the informal sector have more flexibility in business operations. However, in Fiji, female market vendors and farmers tend to have only small savings, which are not enough to mitigate more than 1 or 2 weeks of a downturn in income (COVID-19 Response Gender Working Group 2020). Workers in the informal economy are at risk because they do not have employment contracts, leading to job insecurity in the face of economic uncertainty caused by the pandemic. They also do not have access to social protection such as sick leave, unemployment benefits, or COVID-19 relief benefits; and authorities may see their work as unimportant, less productive, or that they are involved in illegal activities (Pacific Peoples' Partnership 2020).

Women entrepreneurs and women-owned micro, small, and medium-sized enterprises have been negatively affected by increases in unpaid care work responsibilities during the pandemic. School closures and the need to look after and educate children at home, coupled with caring for sick family members, have reduced the amount of time that women can spend on income-generating activities, including managing a business, due to social norms around unpaid care work (ADB 2020c; UNESCAP 2020b). In Fiji, a report in July 2020 from the DFAT-funded Market Development Facility found that 60% of women business owners experienced difficulties in balancing their work and home responsibilities because of the COVID-19 pandemic (Pacific Women Shaping Pacific Development 2021b). Globally, for those working in professional jobs and working remotely, reductions in productivity due to increased unpaid care work responsibilities may have put jobs at risk, which could worsen gender gaps in senior leadership in the future (Asia Foundation 2021).

Gendered barriers in access to finance have worsened the COVID-19 pandemic's impact on women entrepreneurs. All MSMEs are likely to have faced challenges in accessing finance to recover from the effects of the COVID-19 pandemic. However, women are likely to have faced further challenges due to existing barriers such as lower levels of assets (ADB 2020c). The 2020 PTI business monitor survey found that 65% of women-owned businesses needed financial support at the time of the survey (July 2020, 4 months into the pandemic) compared to 49% of male-owned businesses (PTI 2020). Thoughout 2021, 58% of women-owned businesses needed financial support compared to 54% of male-owned businesses.

Women entrepreneurs use digital technologies to cope with the COVID-19 pandemic, but a digital gender gap exists, and some women entrepreneurs are at risk of being left behind. Digital technologies are a key asset for women's economic empowerment. However, women have less access to digital technologies and less digital skills than men, which limits their access to accurate information on COVID-19 (Pacific Women Shaping Pacific Development 2020). There is some evidence that women who have access to digital technologies are using these to supplement their reduced incomes. In Fiji, a Facebook page created on 21 April 2020 had gained over 114,000 members within 2 weeks, a large majority of whom were women. The page encourages non-cash trading and bartering of items such as agricultural produce, groceries, and household items; and this practice has been replicated in other Pacific island countries, which suggests that women are adapting to earning income online (Pacific Islands Forum Secretariat 2020). Women entrepreneurs have also changed the direction of their businesses by producing face masks and doing home delivery (Pacific Islands Forum Secretariat 2020), as well as reducing hours, wages and/or operating costs (CIPE 2021).

There is no evidence on how the COVID-19 pandemic has affected the voice and agency of women entrepreneurs, and there is mixed evidence on their confidence levels. Both the 2020 and 2021 Pacific Business Monitor Surveys found that female business owners are significantly less confident than male business owners that their business will survive the COVID-19 crisis (Figure 14). In July 2020, they were more uncertain about when their businesses will return to pre-COVID-19 revenue levels (32% vs. 17%) (Figure 15) (PTI 2020). However, the overall rating of female business owners feeling worried over the previous 2 weeks before the July 2020 survey was more consistent with that of male business owners (Figure 16) (PTI 2020). In Papua New Guinea, a survey of 144 women

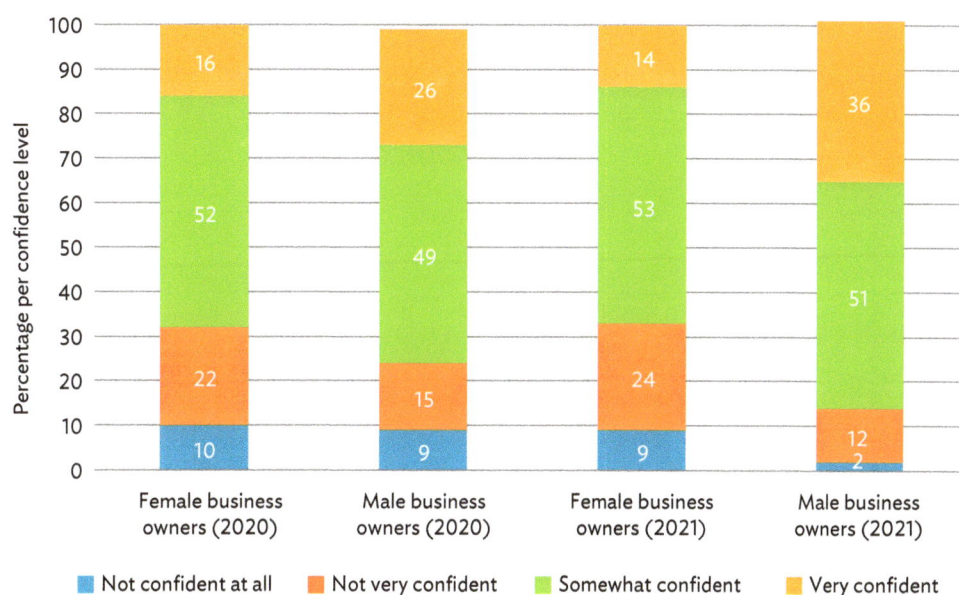

Figure 14: Confidence of Female and Male Business Owners in Business Survival After the COVID-19 Pandemic

Sources: PTI (2020; 2021).

entrepreneurs found that 42.4% felt more confident, compared with 31.9% less confident, in the survival of their business as a result of the COVID-19 pandemic (CIPE 2021). For many of the women respondents, this increase in confidence came from seeing their businesses surviving the pandemic despite significant challenges (CIPE 2021).

Figure 15: Business Owner Predictions for When Revenues Will Return to Pre-COVID-19 Levels (July 2020)

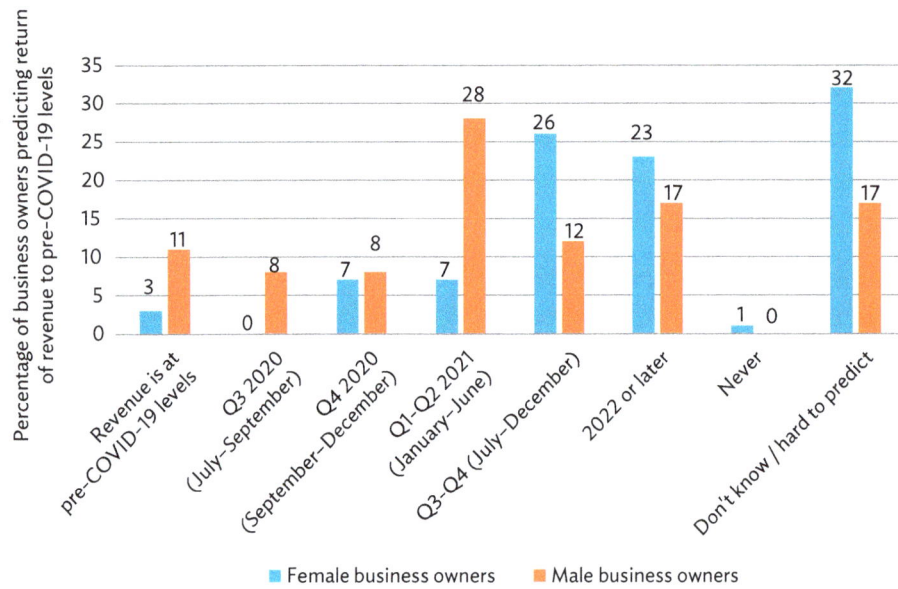

COVID-19 = coronavirus disease, Q = quarter.
Source: PTI (2020).

Figure 16: Percentage of Business Owners Who Felt Worried in the 2 Weeks Prior to the Survey (June/July 2020)

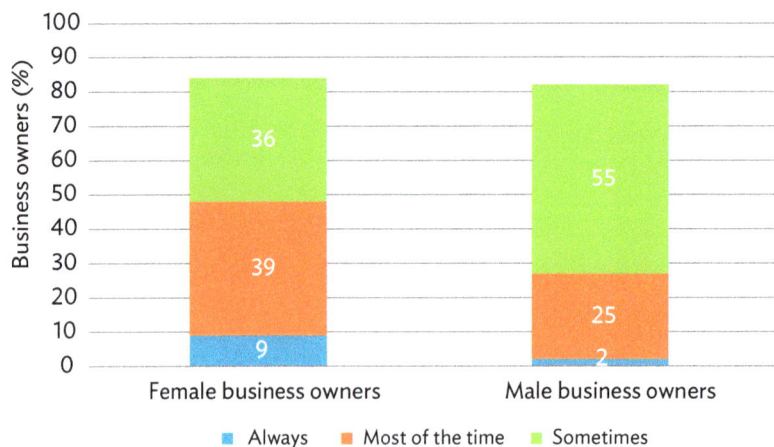

Source: PTI (2020).

How effective have government stimulus or support packages been in accounting for the needs of women entrepreneurs and women-owned micro, small, and medium-sized enterprises, and in mitigating the impact of the COVID-19 pandemic?

Given the differentiated impacts of the COVID-19 pandemic on women, government responses need to be gender-responsive. While many governments in the Pacific adopted at least one gender-responsive measure, most of these measures addressed violence against women. Fewer countries adopted measures targeting women's economic security or unpaid care work.[27] Some economic measures have been gender unaware. For example, many governments have allowed citizens to access their provident or pension funds, which can smooth income over the short term but may have some long-term consequences at retirement age, particularly for women who are likely to have lower pension savings and live longer. A good example of a gender-responsive government response was in Tuvalu. A rapid gender analysis in May 2020 by the Gender Affairs Department found that women were more likely to have lost their incomes; this has led to a recommendation that future financial support be given to households where women's income had dropped (Tuvalu Gender Affairs Department 2020).

Women-owned micro, small, and medium-sized enterprises are struggling to access COVID-19 government support packages. According to PTI (2020), 65% of women-owned MSMEs report that there are barriers to undertaking initiatives supporting their businesses—nearly double the rate reported by male-owned MSMEs (Figure 17).

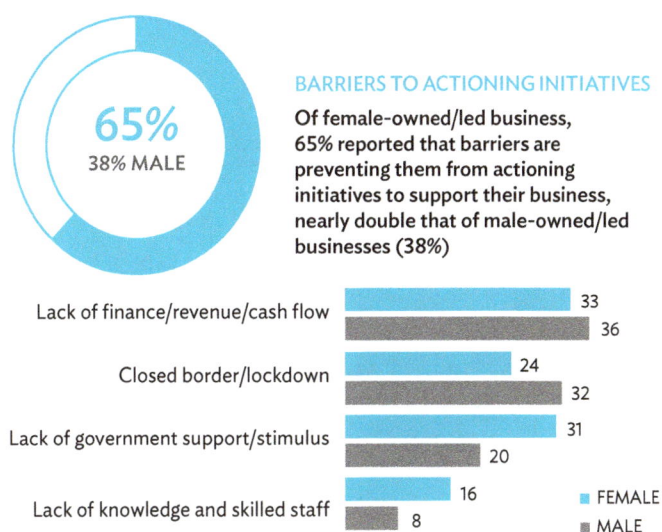

Figure 17: Barriers to Actioning Initiatives to Support Businesses (July 2020)

65%
38% MALE

BARRIERS TO ACTIONING INITIATIVES

Of female-owned/led business, 65% reported that barriers are preventing them from actioning initiatives to support their business, nearly double that of male-owned/led businesses (38%)

Barrier	FEMALE	MALE
Lack of finance/revenue/cash flow	33	36
Closed border/lockdown	24	32
Lack of government support/stimulus	31	20
Lack of knowledge and skilled staff	16	8

Source: PTI (2020).

27   UNDP. COVID-19 Global Gender Response Tracker.: https://data.undp.org/gendertracker/.

In a mid-2021 survey of 144 women entrepreneurs in Papua New Guinea, 98% of respondents had not accessed financial assistance, with 75.2% stating that they did not know it was available (CIPE 2021). For the three people who had accessed financial assistance, the first one received a private bank loan, the second one received a government-sponsored loan, and the third one received a form of assistance which was not a loan (CIPE 2021).

There are some promising examples of regional COVID-19 support interventions for women entrepreneurs, but evidence is not yet available on their impact. The Pacific Islands Forum Secretariat (2020) notes that in some Pacific island countries, the governments are reaching the informal economy, which mostly comprises women MSMEs, through one-off payments. However, these amounts are often too low to meet their needs (Pacific Islands Forum Secretariat 2020). For instance, in Fiji, those with a street hawker or trader license in a lockdown area are entitled to a $150 one-off government relief payment (KPMG 2020). The Pacific Islands Forum Secretariat (2020) also notes that approaches to women's economic empowerment such as the "family teams" approach, flexible funding, and business improvisation to adapt to the "new normal" are being scaled up in the region.[28]

National government stimulus packages for women-owned micro, small, and medium-sized enterprises tend to focus on prioritizing credit. For instance, the government stimulus package in the Federated States of Micronesia includes credit to at least 200 MSMEs with 50% of the loan amount given to women-owned MSMEs. In Palau, concessional loans are given to 100 private firms with women-owned firms as a priority (ADB 2020b). In Fiji, the government has increased its guarantee on new MSME loans with a focus on highly impacted groups. The Government of Fiji also increased the total funding for the MSME Credit Guarantee scheme to $9 million and widened the definition of SMEs to an annual turnover limit of $1.25 million to capture larger businesses (Dahal and Wagle 2020). The scheme guarantees to pay back defaulted loans for MSMEs up to a limit of $60,000 per business or $75,000 for women-owned MSMEs or businesses in the agriculture, forestry, or fisheries sector (Dahal and Wagle 2020). These types of government stimulus packages tend to require businesses to be registered, thereby excluding the many women-owned businesses in the informal economy. However, in Tonga, the women's movement successfully lobbied the government for informal businesses to also be able to access the second round of government assistance (ILO 2021d). No evidence is currently available on the effectiveness of these measures.

Key Evidence Gaps

What do we know about what has worked and has not worked for women's economic empowerment in development partner programs in the Pacific?

There have been a range of large development partner programs addressing women's economic empowerment in the Pacific in recent years (Table 6). The strength of the evidence available on what has worked and has not worked is mixed. For example, for the Pacific Women Shaping Development program, there is a publicly available 3-year evaluation report (ITAD 2017) and a 6-year evaluation report (DFAT 2020), both using qualitative and quantitative methodologies. However, for the Market Development Facility program, no independent evidence on what has worked and has not worked was available. There is a lack of more rigorous methodologies such as randomized controlled trials on the impacts of large development partner programs.

---

[28] The "family teams" approach encourages male and female members of families to work together, using four workshops: (i) working as a family team for family goals, (ii) planning the family farm as a team, (iii) feeding the family team, and (iv) communicating and making decision as a family team (Mikhailovich and Pamphilon 2016).

Table 6: Large Regional Programs Addressing Women's Economic Empowerment in the Pacific

Pacific Women Shaping Pacific Development[a] Development partner: DFAT Implementation period: 2012–2021 Budget: A$320 million	The program found that social norms and cultural practices hinder women's economic empowerment (e.g., biases against women leaders). Evidence from the program suggests that what works are • local organizations leading the change; • supporting collectives and cooperatives to empower women and increase their incomes; • taking a multipronged approach to developing women's knowledge and skills to expand their economic opportunities (e.g., using a combination of training and industry networking activities); • supporting women in both the formal and informal economies; and • building the capacity of local organizations to establish linkages with government and industry.
Market Development Facility[b] Development partner: DFAT Implementation period: 2011–2022 Budget: Phase I—$36 million Phase II—not clear	The program, which operates in Fiji, Pakistan, Papua New Guinea, Sri Lanka, and Timor-Leste, lists lessons learned on women's economic empowerment: • build strategic partnerships with companies that have the capacity to employ women • update and adjust company policies to allow for more flexibility for female workers including flexible working hours • improve access to information in family businesses for informed decision-making by female entrepreneurs • develop support networks for female workers to reduce stigma around women working outside the home.
Pacific Private Sector Development Initiative (PPSDI)[c] Development partner: ADB, DFAT, MFAT Implementation period: 2007–ongoing Budget: Phase IV—$30 million	The program has added a focus on women's economic empowerment during the third phase. Prior to this, PPSDI had some success for example through including women in the Solar Power Development Project in Solomon Islands, however the women's economic empowerment element was not mainstreamed and there was an focus on standalone pilots and programming. In phase IV, the Economic Empowerment of Women (EEOW) has become a dedicated focus area with a twin-track approach of mainstreaming EEOW across all PPSDI focus areas and standalone EEOW activities. Phase IV EEOW programming focuses on five thematic areas: (i) women in business leadership, (ii) the informal economy, (iii) access to finance, (iv) business enabling environment, and (v) women in tourism.
Pacific Readiness for Investment in Social Enterprise (RISE)[d] Development partner: DFAT Implementation period: 2016–2021 Budget: A$3 million	The program promoted the development of an impact-investing market across the Pacific, including a focus on women's economic empowerment through gender lens investing. The recently closed program underperformed in supporting the development of a social impact-investing market, but made commendable efforts in promoting gender lens investing, although with limited evidence of the program impact on women's economic empowerment.

continued on next page

Table 6 *continued*

Markets for Change (M4C) Development partner: DFAT, implemented by UN Women and UNDP Implementation period: 2014–2020 Budget: A$17 million	The program worked toward achieving four outcomes in Fiji, Solomon Islands, and Vanuatu: (i) Inclusive, effective, and representative marketplace groups contributing to gender, social, and economic advancement, the elimination of gender-based discrimination and violence, and the expansion of economic opportunities for women. (ii) Improved socioeconomic security of market vendors. (iii) Local governments and market management that are gender-responsive and accountable to women market vendors' needs. (iv) Improved physical infrastructure and operating systems, making markets more sustainable, resilient to disaster risks and climate change, safer, and more accessible. The program was found to be effective overall but only somewhat effective in supporting women's economic empowerment. While the program was effective in supporting women market vendors' advancement, there was a lack of emphasis on increasing their control over incomes and assets.

ADB = Asian Development Bank, DFAT = Department of Foreign Affairs and Trade of Australia, PPSDI = Pacific Private Sector Development Initiative, UNDP = United Nations Development Programme.

a *Pacific Women* was implemented across 14 Pacific island countries and partnered with governments, local and international nongovernment organizations, the private sector, and others on more than 180 gender equality initiatives. The focus was on ending violence against women and girls, women's economic empowerment, leadership and decision making, and enhancing agency.

b *Market Development Facility* is a multicountry initiative funded by the Government of Australia, which promotes sustainable economic development through market and system change.

c *PPSDI* supports reforms to reduce constraints to doing business, incentivize entrepreneurship and investment, foster new business models, and remove barriers to women's full participation in the economy.

d *Pacific RISE* was designed to pilot and facilitate a social impact market in the Pacific. The program worked with investors and intermediaries to pilot new ways of attracting appropriate capital for investment in social enterprises.

Sources: ADB (2018), DFAT (2020), Fleming and Tabualevu (2018), Hilton et al. (2021), Market Development Facility (2020), Pacific Women Shaping Pacific Development (2021c).

Several lessons have been learned on what works for women's economic empowerment in the Pacific, both from within these programs and elsewhere:

(i) **Strategic partnerships with the government and the private sector can lead to improvements in the working conditions of women employees.** There are early signs that interventions that have partnered with the private sector to improve workplace policies, such as Waka Mere in Solomon Islands and Bel isi in Papua New Guinea, are effective in addressing violence in the workplace (IFC 2019c; IFC 2021).

(ii) **Disrupting harmful social norms is important for women's economic empowerment.** Promising approaches have emphasized the need for local groups to be the ones leading the change. The Pacific Women Shaping Pacific Development program used concurrent approaches, including research and adaptive programming, to understand the dynamics affecting gender inequality, building the capacity of national women's organizations to support policy reform, and supporting coalitions and catalytic women leaders to foster local solutions for change (Pacific Women Shaping Pacific Development 2021c).

(iii) **The "family teams" approach has been successful in encouraging more gender-equitable farming practices in the Pacific region.** It was originally implemented in Papua New Guinea through the CARE Coffee Industry Strengthening Project and the Australian Center for International Agricultural Research (ACIAR) Papua New Guinea Women Smallholders Business Project. The CARE project has led to women's participation in coffee-related extension services increasing from under 5% to 33%–35%, a greater share in financial decision-making between partners, and increases in savings and assets (CARE Australia 2016). The ACIAR project has led to increased production in farms, changed attitudes and practices about gender roles in agriculture, and more equitable decision-making (Mikhailovich and Pamphilon 2016). Lessons learned from the "family teams" approach include adopting a gender-inclusive approach to avoid increased risk of GBV and developing effective partnership and engagement strategies with diverse organizations (Pacific Women Shaping Pacific Development 2017). The "family teams" approach has now been extended to multiple organizations across Polynesia and Melanesia (Pacific Islands Forum Secretariat 2020).

Financial inclusion initiatives in the region have had some success. Tugeda Tude fo Tumoro (TTFT) in Solomon Islands has led to women having greater control of their finances and feeling more control over their own and their families' lives (Pacific Women Shaping Pacific Development 2017). The United Nations Capital Development Fund (UNCDF) Pacific Financial Inclusion Program has increased bank account ownership among women across the Pacific and delivered financial literacy training (PFIP 2016). Lessons learned for financial inclusion initiatives in the region include

(i)   how public–private partnerships can be effective for scaling up service provision and women-targeted products;

(ii)   how integrating women's leadership development into financial inclusion projects can increase women's confidence and skills that results in greater community support for women's leadership;

(iii)   the importance of engaging with male leaders to build their support for women's savings club activities; and

(iv)   how mobile banking services can increase women's independence, privacy, control, and decision-making over financial resources. Interest rates for microfinance are high, thus the use of savings and other informal loans are likely to continue as the main source of finance for women-led MSMEs (Pacific Women Shaping Pacific Development 2017).

Fintech solutions are more limited in the Pacific than in high-income settings, and little is known about how innovations can drive women's economic empowerment. In Samoa, the United Nations Economic and Social Commission for Asia and the Pacific and the UNCDF have been supporting SkyEye, a geographic information system developer, in developing a payments gateway to facilitate a digital interoperable payments system and allow payments to easily flow between banks and mobile money platforms. In a few years, there should be some documented lessons learned on how digitization of payments supports women-led MSMEs to document cash flows and how financial institutions can use its data to make informed lending decisions (UNESCAP and UNCDF 2020). There is also ongoing work on fintech solutions through ADB's programs including the PPSDI Phase IV program.

What is the strength of evidence of women's economic empowerment themes and concepts in the Pacific? How does evidence on women's economic empowerment vary across different geographies?

The strength of the evidence is mixed. Appendix 2 provides an analysis of the strength of the evidence against each research question.[29] Evidence is strongest for Research Question 1 (status and trends of women's economic empowerment in the Pacific), particularly on women's access to assets, services, and opportunities, and key barriers to women's economic empowerment. Evidence is weaker on how climate change is affecting women's

---

[29]   The strength of the evidence was assessed based on the categorization from DFID (2013).

economic empowerment. Evidence is mixed on how women are formalizing and expanding businesses, with strong evidence on the key barriers, status, and trends in women-owned MSMEs, but no evidence on the risks to formalizing women-owned MSMEs. The strength on the evidence of the intersections between women's economic empowerment and violence against women and girls is medium, while there is limited evidence on the effectiveness of interventions. The strength of the evidence is also mixed on the impacts of the COVID-19 pandemic on women-owned MSMEs, and there is no evidence currently available on the effectiveness of government interventions.

The amount of evidence available on women's economic empowerment varies across the Pacific. Much of the evidence found was regional and therefore often included countries that are not ADB developing member countries, or even included the wider Asia and Pacific region or Indo-Pacific region. Even when the data is aggregated at the Pacific level, it is not always useful as there are significant differences among countries, for which the data become obscured. Among Pacific island countries, most of the evidence found was for those that have bigger population—Fiji, Papua New Guinea, Samoa, and Solomon Islands. Evidence was lacking for the Marshall Islands, Nauru, Palau, Tonga, and Tuvalu, and in particular Niue, where only two relevant studies were found.

What methodologies are used and not used to assess women's economic empowerment in the Pacific, and how methodologically robust are these studies?

Most studies used a mixed-methods approach. Surveys, key informant interviews, focus group discussions, and desk-based research were the most frequently used forms of data collection. Research participants were usually women entrepreneurs, community members, employees of private sector companies, key stakeholders from government, staff from civil society organizations, or senior management of private sector companies. Sample sizes varied, with the largest sample size being the 2,650 people who took part in a World Bank phone survey about COVID-19 in Solomon Islands (World Bank 2020b). Larger scale surveys and information on statistical significance are absent, although perhaps this is not surprising given the small population sizes in the Pacific. Other methodologies used included ethnographic studies, legal and economic analyses, and participatory research approaches. Robust quantitative methodologies, such as randomized controlled trials to test the effectiveness of interventions, are absent.

Tables 7 and 8 show the methodologies found in the 267 documents in the research coding matrix. Table 7 gives information about the types of qualitative and quantitative methodologies used. Table 8 gives information about the sample sizes, however, the distinction between interviewees and survey participants was not always clear so the figures should be read as approximations.

Table 7: Methodologies Used in Studies

Methodology	Number of Documents
Methodology not included	43
Desk-based research	100
Survey(s)	51
Interviews	66
Focus group discussions	31
Ethnographic studies	4
Participatory research	8
Evaluations	14
Randomized control trials	0

Note: The total in this table does not add up to the 267 documents reviewed as one study can have multiple methodologies.
Source: Authors.

Table 8: Sample Sizes

Average (mean) number of interviews (for studies using interviews)	66
Average (mean) number of survey participants (for studies using surveys)	666

Source: Authors.

What do we not know about the status and trends of women's entrepreneurship and women-owned micro, small, and medium-sized enterprises in the Pacific?

Several evidence gaps exist against our research questions (a full list is shown in Appendix 2). There is limited evidence from Pacific island countries that have smaller populations, such as Niue, across all the research questions. Gaps are found against the following research questions:

RQ1: What are the status and trends of women's economic empowerment in the Pacific?

- Effects of climate change on women entrepreneurs and women-owned MSMEs
- Women entrepreneurs working in the digital sector

RQ2: How are women owning, formalizing, and expanding their businesses?

- How women-owned MSMEs in the formal sector are expanding
- Sex-disaggregated business ownership in industries directly using natural resources, such as farming, fishing, and mining industries
- Risks or potential risks for women in the formalization of their MSMEs, and how to mitigate them
- Who is providing capital for and investing into women-owned businesses and how this has changed
- Status of social impact investing and gender lens investing

RQ3: What is the association between women's economic empowerment and violence against women and girls for women entrepreneurs and women-owned MSMEs in the Pacific?

- Impacts of economic abuse on women entrepreneurs and women-owned MSMEs
- How online violence and abuse can act as barriers to women's labor force participation and progression
- Impacts of reproductive coercion on women entrepreneurs and women-owned MSMEs
- Effectiveness of interventions addressing violence against women and girls by governments, development partners, civil society, or the private sector for women entrepreneurs and women-owned MSMEs

RQ4: How has the COVID-19 pandemic affected women's economic empowerment in the Pacific?

- Effectiveness of COVID-19 government interventions for women's economic empowerment and women-owned MSMEs.

Further gaps from the research that are not directly related to the research questions are:

- Data and evidence on socially inclusive women's economic empowerment, such as targeting women with disabilities, older women, and LBTQIA+
- Approaches to working with men in the Pacific island countries for women's economic empowerment

- The gendered dimensions of remittances and how they can be used as a tool for women's economic empowerment

- How conflict and post-conflict settings have affected women's economic empowerment in the Pacific

- Barriers that women-led MSMEs firms face in cross-border trade

- The status and trends of women working in the digital sector

To what extent is regional and national data on economic development disaggregated by sex and other intersectional aspects of identity, at the individual level?

Regional data. The Pacific Data Hub; World Bank Gender data portal; Women, Business and the Law; and ILO Statistics all have data according to relevant women's economic empowerment indicators. Also, IFC has MSME Finance Gap data that reports finance gaps for micro-sized businesses and SMEs, disaggregated by sex. For Pacific data hub, there are few Pacific island countries where there is relevant data. For example, time spent on unpaid care work is only reported for Fiji and account ownership at a financial institution or mobile money service provider is only reported for Fiji and Vanuatu. The Cook Islands and the Federated States of Micronesia have sex-disaggregated data for various types of work in the informal economy in the Pacific data hub, which is surprising given the small size of these economies.

National data. Several countries have undertaken economic surveys that are at par with global standards, including sex-disaggregated data, since 2010. These include:

Table 9: Completion of Recent National Economic Surveys

	Cook Islands	Federated States of Micronesia	Fiji	Kiribati	Marshall Islands	Nauru	Niue	Palau	Papua New Guinea	Samoa	Solomon Islands	Tonga	Tuvalu	Vanuatu
Demographic Health Surveys (DHS)	X	X	X	X	X	X	X	X	2016–2018	2019–2020	X	X	X	X
Household Income and Expenditure Surveys (HIES)	2015–2016	2013–2014	X	X	X	2012–2013	2015–2016	2014	2010	X	2012–2013	X	2016	X
Labor Force Surveys	2019	X	X	X	X	X	X	X	X	2017	X	2018	X	X
Multiple Indicator Cluster Surveys (MICS)	X	X	X	2018–2019	X	X	X	X	X	2019–2020	X	2019	2019–2020	X

continued on next page

Table 9 *continued*

	Cook Islands	Federated States of Micronesia	Fiji	Kiribati	Marshall Islands	Nauru	Niue	Palau	Papua New Guinea	Samoa	Solomon Islands	Tonga	Tuvalu	Vanuatu
World Bank enterprise surveys	X	X	X	X	X	X	X	X	2015	X	2015	X	X	X

Source: Authors.

Often Pacific island countries are not included in relevant global databases because the data has not been collected. Table 10 shows which countries are included and excluded from various databases.

Table 10: Inclusion and Exclusion of Pacific Island Countries from Global Databases

	Cook Islands	Federated States of Micronesia	Fiji	Kiribati	Marshall Islands	Nauru	Niue	Palau	Papua New Guinea	Samoa	Solomon Islands	Tonga	Tuvalu	Vanuatu
Global Entrepreneurship Monitor	X	X	X	X	X	X	X	X	X	X	X	✓	X	✓
ILO sex-disaggregated statistics on decent work	✓	✓	✓	✓	✓	✓	X	✓	✓	✓	✓	✓	✓	✓
OECD's Gender, Institutions and Development database[a]	X	X	✓	X	X	X	X	X	✓	✓	✓	X	X	X
United Nations Human Development Data	X	✓	✓	✓	✓	X	X	✓	✓	✓	✓	✓	X	✓
World Economic Forum's Global Gender Gap Index	X	X	✓	X	X	X	X	X	✓	X	X	X	X	✓
World Bank's MSME Finance Gap database	X	✓	✓	X	X	X	X	X	✓	✓	✓	✓	X	✓
World Bank's Women, Business and the Law database	X	✓	✓	✓	✓	X	X	✓	✓	✓	✓	✓	X	✓

X = excluded from the database, ✓ = included in the database

ILO = International Labour Organization; MSME = micro, small, and medium-sized enterprise, OECD = Organisation for Economic Co-operation and Development.

[a] The Gender, Institutions and Development database feeds into the established Social Institutions and Gender Index (SIGI).

Source: Authors.

Pacific island countries may be included in other global databases, but data against specific indicators is missing. For example, under the Asia–Pacific SDG Data Portal, for the Cook Islands, the Federated States of Micronesia, the Marshall Islands, Nauru, Niue, Samoa, and Solomon Islands, data is missing against women's share of employment in managerial positions and middle- and senior-management. In the World Bank Gender Data portal, data is also missing for all Pacific island countries against many indicators (e.g., percentage of women who own land, a house jointly, alone, both).

Some national data is disaggregated by other intersectional aspects of identity. Rural–urban disaggregation and/or disaggregation by age is more common than data disaggregated by disability status.

To what extent is data informing policy on women's economic empowerment, especially for women entrepreneurs and women-owned micro, small, and medium-sized enterprises?

There is little information available on how data is informing policy on women's economic empowerment for women entrepreneurs and women-owned micro, small, and medium-sized enterprises. In Fiji, data from a 2010/2011 national survey found that 1 in 5 women had experienced sexual harassment in the workplace, and this data informed a lobbying campaign by the Fiji Women's Rights Movement. This campaign was a significant factor in influencing the Government of Fiji to ratify the international treaty on violence and harassment in the workplace (ILO Convention 190) in June 2021 (Center for Women's Global Leadership 2021). In Papua New Guinea, data on women's formal businesses is "piecemeal and often anecdotal" (Nagarajan 2021: 2), which does not provide reliable data to inform policy.

4 Conclusions and Recommendations

Woman selling bread.

There are barriers to women's economic participation and agency. Women's labor market participation is lower than men's, and women are predominantly in the informal economy. A high percentage of women are participating in the ownership of businesses, but these tend to be small and informal. Worsening climate change outcomes and the COVID-19 pandemic affect women-owned businesses disproportionately, and women have less access to digital technology and mobile banking. Social and gender norms are a major constraint to women's economic empowerment as they dictate that women bear the burden of unpaid domestic care work, constrain their access to and ownership of resources and assets, limit their voice and agency, and make them vulnerable to violence at home and in the workplace.

The enabling environment has improved over the years but there are still significant gaps in many Pacific island countries, and policy implementation has been slow. There are evidence gaps in childcare policy; understanding of gender relations (rather than a focus on women); and ensuring incentives for business establishment, formalization, and expansion through a progressive tax system. Development partners have significantly increased their focus on women's economic empowerment in the last decade. Do No Harm strategies have been adopted, as well as a two-pronged approach to mainstreaming gender equality in investment projects such as water supply and sanitation, infrastructure, and rural development projects (specially to reduce the burden of women's work). They also have invested in projects that promote women's leadership, voice, economic empowerment, and ending violence against women and girls. However, even when there have been positive changes to policy and legislation, there are usually limited capacity, resources, or desire to fully implement these changes. While men continue to dominate the leadership and decision-making positions across government and the private sector, social norms that limit women's economic opportunities will continue to inform decision-making and practices in systems, policies, and processes.

A concerted effort from governments, the private sector, civil society, and development partners has great potential to increase women's economic empowerment in the Pacific. In Solomon Islands, evidence shows that increasing women's access to financial products leads to greater bargaining power in household decision-making and to the establishment of women-owned businesses (Pacific Financial Inclusion Program 2016). There is also strong evidence on the potential of digital technologies to improve business outcomes for women, through reaching new markets and accessing financial services (GSMA 2014; FAO and SPC 2019; UNESCAP 2020b). Yet they also pose new risks with women being left behind and exposed to new forms of violence and exploitation. Increasing the effectiveness of policies, projects, and interventions by governments and development partners requires access to more and better data on trends, and on what works and what does not.

Recommendations

In this section, recommendations are discussed according to those that relate to research, policy, and program. Appendix 3 maps out the recommendations to each of the research questions, together with a summary of the strength of evidence.

Areas for further research

It is crucial that more independent and rigorous independent evaluation of women's economic empowerment interventions are carried out to understand what works in the region. A stronger evidence base will naturally lead to more informed and potentially effective interventions to ensure women's economic empowerment. The full set of research gaps are provided in Section 3.5, and below are the most pertinent research gaps identified from this literature review:

High Priority

- **Status and trends of women-owned micro, small, and medium-sized enterprises and women entrepreneurs in Pacific island countries that have smaller populations.** Much of the current evidence is dominated by Fiji, Papua New Guinea, Solomon Islands, and Samoa; and regional statistics often obscure the situation of countries that have smaller populations. More evidence is needed from countries such as the Cook Islands, Niue, the Marshall Islands, Palau, and Tuvalu. There does not seem to be an association with higher income countries having more data and studies on women's economic empowerment.

- **Women's economic empowerment status and trends for women from groups that have historically been marginalized more than others.** Examples include women with disabilities, adolescent girls, sexual and gender minorities, ethnic and indigenous minority women, migrants, and those raising children on their own. Poverty and marginalization are likely to run deeper for these groups of women and it is crucial to understand their distinct situation, which can often get missed in aggregate data.

- **Forms of support for women-owned businesses to become more resilient to climate change.** The Pacific is a region that is highly vulnerable to the effects of climate change such as extreme weather events and sea-level rise. The high-profile presence of the Pacific island countries at the 2021 United Nations Climate Change Conference (COP26) underscored these concerns. It is particularly important to gather data on women entrepreneurs in green businesses, what sectors they are working in, and what their business plans are. This would be a prerequisite to targeting specific support and to creating incentives for businesses in the green economy.

- **Effectiveness of COVID-19 government stimulus or support packages aimed at women-owned businesses and women entrepreneurs.** At the time of writing, in addition to the pandemic Pacific island countries had experienced several geophysical and extreme weather events such as typhoons, volcanic eruptions, and tidal waves, which caused further economic shocks. Governments and development partners can learn from these events to help improve future action. This will be important not only for recovery from the COVID-19 pandemic but also for future crises such as economic shocks and the threats of climate change.

Medium Priority

- **Incentives for business formalization and the entry points and mechanisms for expanding formal businesses.** Evidence is stronger on women in the informal economy, but there is little available research about the status of women-owned businesses once they are in the formal economy, and about the process of formalization. It is equally important to know the mechanisms through which women in the formal economy can operate sustainably and can expand their businesses over time. There is a need to understand how access to finance, digital technologies, and diaspora communities, among others, can be used to help women who own formal businesses. Little is known about the most effective incentives for business formalization, and what the risks and benefits of formalization are and the strategies that can be put in place to mitigate any potential negative outcomes.

- **Interconnections between violence against women and girls and women's economic empowerment.** Currently there is a gap in understanding the relationship between women's economic empowerment and intimate partner violence for women-owned MSMEs and women entrepreneurs, including the role of discriminatory social norms and gender roles in the region. There is also a gap in understanding how to design effective interventions that empower women economically while also reducing the risks of violence faced by women entrepreneurs and women-owned MSMEs in their daily lives. Online violence and abuse can act as barriers to women's labor force participation, progression, and business ownership. This is particularly true given the prevalence of social media and the lack of legal protections.

Lower Priority

- **Strategies to influence social norms on women's roles in business.** This review has illuminated how social norms can act as a deterrent to women's business establishment, formalization, and expansion. More knowledge is needed on strategies of changing norms at the community and household level, and how actors can shift these norms over the long term. It is crucial to gain evidence about (i) how governments can change norms through childcare, parental leave, and tax and social protection policies; (ii) the most effective ways for development partners to support in-country stakeholders, such as women's rights organizations and young people, in tapping the potential of social media and innovative technologies to disrupt norms; and (iii) the extent to which the private sector and trade associations can shift norms in the workplace. Identifying successful strategies could be through more rigorous evaluation of previous experience or by monitoring pilot initiatives that are working elsewhere. Methodologies that measure these changes, which are often qualitative in nature, need to be developed. Social norms may vary according to subregion (i.e., Melanesia, Micronesia, and Polynesia).

- **Social protection options for workers in the lower segments of the informal economy, including women-owned informal micro, small, and medium-sized enterprises.** The COVID-19 pandemic has further highlighted the economic precarity of women working within the informal economy, and the evidence is clear that women-owned MSMEs have been disproportionately affected. Business expansion involves a degree of risk, which is not acceptable if the chance of falling into absolute poverty is real. Most countries in the Pacific now have basic social protection systems in place, and many have expanded these as part of their COVID-19 response. Countries continue to build robust social protection systems that are flexible and responsive in times of crisis. However, there is still a gap in developing specific measures to protect the informal sector workers despite their significant contribution to the economy. Options for providing coverage to ensure they can withstand shocks, and recover and grow their businesses, need to be explored.

Policy Recommendations

The following recommendations are for policy makers in the Pacific region, to be assisted by ADB and other stakeholders in the development community:

High Priority

- **Repeal legislation that prohibits women from certain types of work.** Currently, there are restrictions on the types of jobs that women can take in Vanuatu, Solomon Islands, Papua New Guinea, and Fiji, such as work at night or work considered too dangerous. However, these laws limit the employment of women workers and conflict with laws that promote equal employment opportunities for all. To address safety concerns, protection measures for workers can be provided, such as laws giving all night workers adequate and reasonable facilities like sleeping or resting quarters in the establishment and transportation to and from work. Similarly, there should be national policies and action plans on occupational health. Essential interventions to prevent and control occupational and work-related injuries and diseases and occupational health services should also be scaled up. Policies and interventions should recognize and account for the different physical and psychological risks that women and men can be exposed to. From 2014 to 2017, the Pacific Women Shaping Pacific Development implemented the IFC-funded Strengthening Business Coalitions for Women and Economic Empowerment Partnership with a private sector project in Papua New Guinea. As a result, the Papua New Guinea Business Coalition for Women has developed the Gender Smart Safety Resources for its members, which cover workplace safety and safety audit systems that are used to promote continuous improvements on work sites. These were developed as some women were overlooked for job opportunities as employers believed they could not guarantee workplace safety for women (Pacific Women Shaping Pacific Development 2018).

- **Regulators, such as central banks or banking authorities, to require sex-disaggregated data to be collected, publicly released and reported.** The collection and use of national-level, sex-disaggregated datasets on the supply side are lacking (GBA 2019). The rationale for such a requirement first needs to be established by demonstrating the business case for taking a more gender-sensitive approach to provision of financial services in the Pacific building on experience elsewhere. There should also be a collaborative process to determine the data required and address the challenges to collecting and reporting data with the required segmentation. It would require updates and changes to the management information systems so that they are set up to capture the data. Data, such as the definition of women-owned MSMEs, should be based on international standards; it should also be accurate so that there are no double counting of accounts (GBA 2019). Sufficient time should be provided to harmonize standards and make changes to the management information system. A proper time frame is to be allocated for testing, validating, and cleaning the data collected. Once the data is disseminated, financial service providers are to be encouraged to use the data in addressing the needs of women, in designing and marketing products, and in undertaking further gender-responsive market research (AFI 2020). AFI (2020) provides templates for regulated financial institutions to report sex-disaggregated data to central banks.

Medium Priority

- **Ratify ILO Convention No. 190 on violence and harassment in the world of work and adopt and enforce sexual harassment legislation and policies in employment.** ILO C190 is the first international treaty to recognize the right of everyone to a world of work free from violence and harassment, including gender-based violence and harassment. It represents a historic opportunity to shape the future of work based on dignity and respect for all (ILO 2022). Regional forums in the Pacific have already started discussing this (see ILO 2021a), and social dialogue is an important step in building a sense of ownership and will likely result in ensuring effective implementation (ILO 2021c). Fiji is one out of 25 countries globally where C190 has been ratified. Samoa has made a commitment to ratify, and Tonga has established a sexual harassment policy for public sector workers. With the regional commitment starting to build, support is needed to identify changes that need to be made in national laws and policies to comply with the convention. Once the convention is ratified and legislations regarding sexual harassments and employment policies have been adopted, continued support is needed to build awareness of these legal changes, establish the organizational structure and responsibilities to monitor compliance, and hold offenders accountable. This could be done alongside strengthening the enforcement of existing domestic violence legislation.

- **Reform tax, finance, and licensing policies and systems to remove barriers and disincentives for women-owned businesses to formalize.** Pacific island countries should systematically analyze the impact of tax administration or compliance on gender, with the design of explicit tax biases to reduce gender inequalities (OECD 2022). This could include gender responsive policies integrated into tax regulations such as lower tax rates for micro- and small-sized businesses, which women disproportionately own. Taxes for the first few years for informal businesses that choose to formalize can also be waived. Digital technologies can be harnessed like in the case of Tonga, where one can apply for a business license online, which reduces the risk of corruption and takes less time. Paper forms should continue to exist for those that do not have an internet connection. Simplification of the business registration process has increased registration of women's businesses in Uganda and Viet Nam.[30] Policy analysis and pilot programs could help identify policies that would allow formalization to bring long-term benefits to businesses. They could also help in determining the risks that need to be mitigated. It may be more advantageous for some women-owned businesses to remain in the informal economy, and the government should provide support to these firms as well.[31] This would entail removing discriminatory laws, promoting legal recognition of informal workers, and widening the coverage of social protection systems to enhance the entitlements of informal workers and entrepreneurs (Chen 2012 and UNHLP 2016 cited in Hearle et al. 2019).[32] There should also be a focus on enacting laws that prohibit discrimination in access to credit based on gender. Pacific island countries can learn from the case of the Marshall Islands—looking at how they did it, applying the lessons learned, and considering the policy impacts. Global literature suggests that laws that prevent women's access to credit are strongly correlated with a firm having a male owner (Islam et al. 2019).

- **Enact parental leave policies that can contribute to changing social norms.** Table 1 demonstrated that many Pacific island countries do not have legislation on the dismissal of pregnant workers and do not have government-funded paid leave of at least 14 weeks available to mothers. Globally, maternity leave has been found to significantly increase women's labor force participation and reduce gender gaps in earnings (Gonzalez et al. 2015). Progressive step changes in parental leave laws may have a "magnet effect" by changing social norms along with the legal reform (see Aldashev et al. 2012).[33]

---

[30] In Uganda, a pilot project to simplify business start-up procedures led to a rapid increase in business registrations and an increase in first-time business owners (33% higher for women than men). Similarly, in Viet Nam, the Enterprise Law 22 simplified business registration procedures so that new enterprises could be registered in an average of 7 days as opposed to 90 days, which led to a considerable expansion in the share of women-owned enterprises of approximately 20% in the 1990s to 33% in 2009 (Kabeer 2012 cited in Congrave et al. 2020)

[31] PPSDI is working on alternative business entities, which may better suit women in the Pacific.

[32] There is increasing recognition of the need for universal forms of social protection but less agreement on what forms these should take or how these can be financed (Chen 2012; Stuart et al. 2018). The viability of extending coverage also differs across contexts, partly depending on the share of informal in total employment (Loayza 2018). Integrated approaches to social protection and taxation are needed, drawing on experiences in Latin America, to encourage extension of rights and social protection to informal workers, without discouraging small businesses from registering or hiring workers through excessive taxation (Stuart et al. 2018).

[33] A study of 31 low- and middle-income countries found that a 1-month increase in the legislated duration of paid maternity leave increased the odds that women and their partners reported that women had more decision-making power by 40% and 66%, respectively. A 1-month increase in the legislated duration of paid maternity leave was associated with 41.5 percentage-point increase in the prevalence of individuals disagreeing with the statement that "when jobs are scarce, men should have more right to a job than women" (Chai et al. 2021).

In Türkiye, as per Article 74 of the 2013 Labor Law, women employees are allowed one-and-a-half-hour nursing leave a day to feed their children under the age of one (IFC 2017). Laws like this that are adapted to the Pacific context would allow women to better balance paid work and unpaid care work duties, and result in greater retention of women in the labor market. It is also important to have a simultaneous focus on paternity leave provisions so that social norms around the gendered division of care work are not reinforced (Chopra and Krishnan 2019). Evidence from analyses of parental leave policies in Germany, Israel, Japan, Poland, Portugal, Sweden, and the United States suggests that legislating exclusive leave for fathers, rather than shared parental leave with mothers, is a crucial factor in securing a high percentage of paternity leave usage (Rocha 2020).

- **Introduce childcare policies to help women who manage their own business in the informal economy, or those who want to return to, or stay at work after having children.** Samman et al. (2016) provide several recommendations on the intersections of women's work and the "global childcare crisis." These include (i) promoting an integrated, multigenerational approach to social protection programming that is sensitive to care responsibilities, including men in care provider agendas; and (ii) investing in better data. For instance, in the Cook Islands during the COVID-19 pandemic, the government provided payments every 2 weeks during school closures for children aged between 0 and 16 years old.[34] Early childhood development (ECD) strategies are already being discussed in regional forums such as the Pacific Early Childhood Development Forums, organized by UNICEF and funded by the Government of New Zealand. ECD provides an entry point for expanding high quality service provision to younger children and extending the hours to help working families. ECD not only helps children's development but also enables women to work. The Pacific Regional Council for Early Childhood Development with Pacific governments need to develop policies to improve and regulate service provision, broaden data and evidence-gathering systems, and explore options for public and/or private sector financing according to their national context to provide services that are affordable for working families. IFC's work on employer provision of childcare, including their work in Fiji, provides a strong business case for further investment by government and the private sector in expanding childcare provision (see IFC 2019a).

- **Promote and legislate equal renumeration for work of equal value in ways that suit national contexts.** This study has found that laws mandating equal renumeration for work of equal value and legislation in the Pacific are the least commonly enacted. Raising awareness of the gender pay gap and its causes is an important starting point to promoting equal pay.[35] Second, the content, scope, and implications of the equal pay principle must be widely understood. Specialized information and training on equal pay can be targeted to labor and employment officials, those in equality or human rights bodies, judges, labor inspectors, human resource managers and consultants, workers and employers and their organizations, as well as women's organizations. Third, equal pay provisions or legislation in line with ILO Convention No. 100 on equal renumeration for work of equal value should be adopted, implemented, and enforced, ensuring that legislation provides for equal pay for work of equal value and not simply equal pay for equal work. Fourth, governments and social partners should promote objective job evaluation methods that are free from gender bias. Last, measures taken to achieve equal pay should be reviewed regularly to assess whether they are still appropriate and effective (ILO 2013a).[36]

---

[34] See Ministry of Internal Affairs. School Closure Support. https://www.intaff.gov.ck/covid19-response-package/family-elderly-children/school-closure-support/.

[35] Possible actions include improving the availability of statistics on renumeration disaggregated by sex; undertaking, encouraging, and supporting research on the gender pay gap, including its causes and evolution; making the reduction of gender pay gap as an explicit point for action to promote gender equality; promoting pay surveys; and ensuring that information on the gender pay gap reaches the public, policy, and decision-making in politics, labor, the economy, government, and civil society.

[36] Actions can be taken in the following areas: collection and analysis of statistical data on renumeration to monitor the gender pay gap over time; collection and analysis of information on the number, nature, and outcome of legal proceedings involving disputes concerning equal pay; review of collective agreements and minimum wages from the perspective of equal renumeration for work of equal value; and case studies, for example on the gender pay gap in specific sectors or for categories of workers, or on the impact of specific policy interventions.

Lower Priority

- **Develop national regulatory frameworks for crowdfunding and peer-to-peer lending.** There should be a dual focus on encouraging financial institutions to accept non-land assets as collateral and also for women-owned MSMEs to draw on funding from nontraditional sources. PPSDI is supporting the setup of national regulatory frameworks for crowdfunding and peer-to-peer lending in Papua New Guinea and Fiji, although work is at the early stage. Emerging economies, such as Malaysia, are developing national regulatory frameworks for crowdfunding, thereby improving access and awareness of this investment opportunity (ADB and Asia Foundation 2018). Securities Commission Malaysia added peer-to-peer regulation to its alternative finance regulatory framework in 2016. By December 2018, 643 MSMEs in Malaysia had raised capital through peer-to-peer platforms with transaction volume rising fourfold since 2017 (Securities Commission Malaysia 2018 cited in World Bank and CCAF 2019). Care should be taken in these platforms to ensure the criteria for women-owned MSMEs seeking investment is equal to that of male-owned MSMEs. Research by World Bank and CCAF (2019) found that the existing national regulatory frameworks tend to prioritize checks on investor exposure, rigorous due diligence on fundraisers, client money protection, and appropriate online marketing standards. To prevent fraud, capital loss, and money laundering, alternative finance supervisors prioritize regulatory sandboxes, have innovation offices, and have active RegTech and/or SupTech programs.[37]

- **Incentivize gender-responsive procurement processes in the public and private sector.** Governments could enact policy and legislative frameworks that explicitly support or actively promote gender-responsive procurement. This could include preferential treatment for women-owned MSMEs such as set asides and targets for total procurement spending per year and other forms of preferential treatment, including gender-responsive clauses in supplier codes of conduct, establishing regular spot-checks and audits, and reporting on gender in supply chains. For example, Tanzania's 2016 Public Procurement Act allocates 30% of government tenders to enterprises led by women, youth, older persons, and people with disabilities (UN Women and ILO 2021). Other examples include using e-procurement systems, building capacity to help women-owned MSMEs apply for government contracts, establishing women-owned business certification, and simplifying administrative procurement and company registration processes.[38] It could also involve buying from gender-responsive enterprises to create more gender-responsive value chains, such as sourcing from suppliers that have a gender balance in the workforce across all levels of seniority and strong gender equality policies, or are committed to recruiting a percentage of women for the awarded contract (Combaz 2018). Governments could publish a database of gender-responsive enterprises to allow private buyers to access the information.[39] This database would help private sector buyers to identify women-owned businesses and invite them to tender bids (UN Women and ADB 2022). To inform scalable practices, companies can roll out a series of pilot projects to learn what works and what does not work.[40] There may be learnings from companies such as Accenture, Citi, Ernst & Young, and Procter & Gamble, who in 2017 all announced a goal to source $100 million each through their supply chains from women enterprises in developing countries. Results from a pilot project suggest these companies saw reputational benefits from this scheme and positive impacts on performance (UN Women and ILO 2021).

---

[37] A regulatory sandbox is a framework that allows FinTech start-ups to test and pilot new products on a small scale in a controlled environment under regulatory supervision. An innovation office is the function within a regulator which engages with- and provides clarification to- innovative financial services providers. SupTech is the use of innovative technologies by regulators to tackle regulatory or supervisory challenges; it is a subset of RegTech, which includes any use of technology to match data to information taxonomies or decision rules, to automate compliance or oversight processes.

[38] Allowing collectives of women informal producers to bid can be effective. For example, in India, the Kagad Kach Patra Kashtakari Panchayat in Pune, and in Colombia, the Asociación Cooperativa de Recicladores de Bogotá, two cooperatives of waste pickers, have bid for and secured municipal contracts to collect, sort, transport, and dispose waste (Klugman and Tyson 2016 cited in Congrave et al. 2020).

[39] Databases of eligible companies that are expanded to include smaller companies would likely include more companies owned by women.

[40] In driving gender-responsive procurement, people, policy, practice, communication, knowledge, and stakeholder management are all important factors to consider. (See guidance note by WEPS 2020).

Program Recommendations

Programs funded by development partners in the Pacific need to use sound evidence to pursue innovative and gender transformative approaches to women's economic empowerment. Current programs are addressing risks, basic needs, and vulnerabilities, as well as building assets, capabilities, and opportunities for women. However, there is now a need to increase the level of ambition to remove systemic barriers to inclusive growth and challenge power imbalances that prevent women from participating, contributing, and benefiting from economic growth (Prosperity Fund, unpublished). Addressing the systemic barriers can have far reaching and multiplying effects. Some proposed program recommendations are as follows:

High Priority

- **Encourage financial institutions to accept non-land assets as collateral and increase uptake of secured transaction frameworks.** The lack of collateral due to a lack of land rights is a major barrier to accessing commercial finance that is crucial for expanding and formalizing businesses. The Federated States of Micronesia, the Marshall Islands, Vanuatu, Solomon Islands, Tonga, Papua New Guinea, Palau, and Fiji have secured transaction frameworks although take-up is limited. Reasons for the limited take-up should be investigated and overcome. Governments should work with financial institutions, trade associations, and women's business networks to raise awareness of the framework.[41] Programs can encourage financial institutions to accept non-land forms of collateral, including personal property, long-term contracts, and invoices and patents. For people who lack sufficient credit history, financial institutions can use alternative credit risk assessment mechanisms such as machine learning and psychometric testing-based risk assessment (Klinger et al. 2013; Alibhai et al. 2018; ADB 2020b). Alternative forms of credit assessment could be information from repayment of utility bills and mobile phone usage (ADB 2018). In Mongolia, LendMN, a fintech provider that lends primarily to women has developed a mobile application that uses artificial intelligence to enable previously underserved customers to get loans without any collateral (ADB 2020c). Useful lessons learned could be gained from the work of PPSDI in its piloting of alternative credit risk mechanisms and support of the establishment of secured transactions frameworks in several Pacific island countries.

- **Work with national statistics agencies and designers of international surveys to improve the quality of existing surveys and include sex-disaggregated questions.** Much of the research on women's economic participation and advancement has been dominated by smaller sample size studies, which are less effective in influencing policy. While it may not be possible to generate large-scale surveys from women business owners due to small populations, it would be possible to include gendered questions on women's economic empowerment and women's entrepreneurship in large-scale quantitative surveys. Evidence suggests the need to (i) adopt a strong mandate from across different government functions to incorporate a gender focus; (ii) establish a multistakeholder task force to set targets, review progress, and make suggestions for strategy and target refinement; (iii) conduct gender sensitization training in government departments and ministries; and (iv) earmark technical assistance funds for modifying systems and processes to improve data quality. Both supply- and demand-side, sex-disaggregated data should be collected, drawing on existing questions in Demographic and Health Surveys, MSME surveys, and World Values Surveys. Once sex-disaggregated data has been collected, ensuring data is published and distributed widely is key (GBA 2019). Using a series of case studies, UNESCAP (2016) outlines several good practices in integrating gender in national statistics systems.

[41] In a preliminary review, ADB (2014) finds that some bankers are unaware of how to use the new framework; most businesses are unaware of the potential for borrowing; and bank regulators do not realize its potential for strengthening bank regulation.

- **Develop and implement targeted measures to help self-employed women restart their businesses that collapsed or are in "survival mode" because of the challenges associated with the COVID-19 pandemic.** This may include training and coaching provision (such as on digital skills to access new markets), incentives for formalization, business plan competitions, lines of credit for women-owned firms, access to credit, and subsidized and state-backed low-interest loans. In the People's Republic of China, Rockcheck Puji Foundation is funding the Supporting Women to Recover from the Socio-Economic Impacts of COVID-19 project, implemented by UN Women China and the All-China Women's Federation. Another program that is supporting women-owned small businesses in the Asia and Pacific region is the Rebuilding Better project, funded by J.P. Morgan Chase Foundation, which was implemented in the urban areas of Thailand, Malaysia, and the Philippines from January 2021 to June 2022. Both projects are delivering training and skills development opportunities, facilitating access to financial services, and assisting women entrepreneurs to take advantage of new and existing market opportunities such as through business continuity plans (ILO 2021c; UN Women 2021). UN Women (2020) provides several recommendations for governments, businesses, development partners, and civil society organizations in supporting women-owned SMEs during the COVID-19 pandemic.

- **Invest in evidence-based programming that aims to shift harmful social norms that sustain violence against women and girls in the world of work, focusing on women entrepreneurs and women-owned micro, small, and medium-sized enterprises.** This is an area for further innovation, with limited research both in the Pacific and globally. It requires careful investigation using rigorous formative and operational research, building on best practices on intervention design on violence against women and girls and women's economic empowerment. Existing evidence suggests that it requires multiple interventions at the individual and community levels and in educational and work settings. In targeting women entrepreneurs, it would be important to involve women's rights organizations, including women's business networks, to ensure messages are culturally appropriate and will not cause further harm to working women.

Medium Priority

- **Building on good practice and experience in the Pacific, work with banks to adjust risk assessment criteria and models in favor of micro, small, and medium-sized enterprises and informal businesses and ensure that financial products and services are adapted to women clients.** There is strong evidence that women are equally as reliable borrowers of capital as men, if not more. Such evidence should be presented to these banking institutions to influence them to take on women clients. Risk assessment criteria should be adapted to ensure they are positive for MSMEs and informal businesses, such as movable assets as collateral. Banks should have information and database management technology to develop risk scoring models, value models, and customer preference models to fully understand the risks and manage the critical moments of the customer life-cycle (IFC 2012b cited in IFC 2013). Consultations with women and their representative groups, and sex-disaggregated data from market research, can be used by banks to adapt financial products and services to overcome the constraints that MSMEs and informal businesses often face (Hearle and Smith 2021). Low-tech yet innovative approaches could be voiced by women as ways to address financial inclusion gaps such as recruiting and training women to deliver financial services and providing branchless banking in remote areas (ADB 2020b). For instance, in Papua New Guinea, the UNCDF Pacific Financial Inclusion Program worked with Women's Microbank Limited (WMBL) to set up six banking points in rural areas where customers use biometric identification and authentication systems. Aimed primarily at women, the establishment of these banking points was a principal factor in raising WMBL's customer base by 65% in one year. Supporting women's groups in raising awareness of the access points was a critical success factor (GPFI 2020 cited in Hearle and Smith 2021).

- **Improve access to and understanding of regulations and official procedures.** This report has found that women have more difficulty in accessing information that is essential for conducting business. Women must rely on officials and government offices for information, rather than on online resources, which leaves them vulnerable to exploitation, corruption, and abuse. Governments need to focus on improving the dissemination of information to women in business across a wide range of accessible channels, including for women with disabilities. Governments could consult and partner with women in business networks and regional bodies such as the Pacific Island Forum and the Pacific Community to determine the most effective communication channels to reach women in all their diversity. To raise awareness on trade facilitation procedures, the World Bank (2020a) recommends the following:

  (i)   Establish (or improve any existing) trade information portal, single window, and/or physical office to more promptly publish and disseminate information on the import and/or export of goods;

  (ii) Keep trade information portals up-to-date;

  (iii) Encourage increased use of online resources, including by border officials;

  (iv) Offer targeted information and capacity building sessions to women workers on the use of electronic systems;

  (v)   Target trading associations to enhance dissemination of information to women;

  (vi) Make sure official legislation is easy to understand; and

  (vii) Publicize official grievance procedures.

- **Support in-country stakeholders to disrupt social norms that act as barriers to women's business and work with men and boys to support women's economic empowerment.** There are three stages to shifting social norms: (i) changing social expectations regarding the desired behavior change among the people who hold that norm in place such as through dispelling misconceptions and promoting public debate; (ii) publicizing the change in attitudes, expectations, and behaviors; and (iii) catalyzing and reinforcing new positive behaviors and norms through rewards, sanctions, and opportunities to conform (Investing in Women 2020). Changing harmful social norms requires strategic harmonized interventions at multiple levels with multiple groups. Development partners could work with media agencies and other private sector institutions to promote positive male and female role models, challenging stereotypes of what is women's work and what is men's work. For example, Ariel India's campaign "See Equal #ShareTheLoad" displayed an alternative version of masculinity, and it had garnered over 64 million views on YouTube at the time of writing this paper.[42] Similarly the government could publicly recognize and reward women in business, especially women in leadership positions. Whatever intervention is decided upon, it is crucial to conduct baseline studies to know the local context, carry out a pilot test, and redevelop and retest the campaign messaging. Campaigns need to be supplemented at the individual, community, and institutional levels with critical reflection, advocacy, and policy work. It is important to reach men in public education and campaigns; best practice suggests that it is important to start working with boys early in their lifetime and to work with girls and women at the same time (Investing in Women 2020).

- **Develop the unpaid and paid care provider economy and infrastructure, such as supporting quality and affordable care services.** Such investment serves the dual purpose of improving the quality of jobs in the largely female-dominated informal domestic work sector and addressing the constraints to women's labor participation at a wider scale (UNHLP 2016; OECD 2019). Good quality childcare services should be affordable and accessible; have opening hours that can accommodate informal workers' long and irregular working hours; encourage parental participation in the running of the childcare center and

---

[42]   When we #SeeEqual, we #ShareTheLoad - YouTube.

establish strong communication between parents and childcare providers; and guarantee that childcare workers receive a living wage, training, and decent working conditions. The childcare service should also offer educational components and learning materials; ensure a connection to a health service that can monitor children's nutrition and development; provide basic infrastructure, good hygiene, and adequate number of skilled staff; and offer nutritious food (ILO and WIEGO 2020). UNICEF (2022) provides some considerations, principles, and guidelines for reopening childcare and early learning services in East Asia and the Pacific after periods of COVID-19 lockdowns, which could be adapted to educational settings for older children.

- **Fund women's business networks in the region and raise their capacity to engage in more diverse activities.** While traditional development partners may fund business networks initially, there should be a transition to government funding to ensure sustainability. These networks can partner with the private sector on areas such as addressing violence experienced by women workers and communicating and supporting women entrepreneurs to access COVID-19 support packages from governments. Training and mentoring should continue to be important functions for these groups, but they should also be influencing governments to implement policies that have positive impact on women's businesses and hold them accountable to commitments made. Hence, political space needs to be created for these networks to participate in policy forums and dialogue on issues that directly affect women's livelihoods (Hearle et al. 2019). Formalization of these networks would ensure greater potential to engage in policy dialogue. It is important that members of women's business networks have representation in industry associations, which often serve as important conduits of business-related information. Development banks could run pilot mentoring schemes to strengthen the business skills of these groups. Tonga Development Bank has an existing program, but it does not target women specifically (ADB 2018).

- **Leverage digital access and increase access to mobile phones for women, accompanied with skills building on digital literacy and scale up promising initiatives.** Actions of stakeholders should be grounded in an understanding of the country-level barriers that women face in owning and using a mobile phone. Barriers can be related to access, affordability, safety and security, knowledge and skills, and the availability of relevant content, products, and services. To help overcome these barriers, GSMA (2021) provides recommendations for mobile operators, internet companies, policy makers and regulators, and the development community. Women-targeted training on digital skills may be needed, as they face more barriers than men in participating in digital literacy programs. Women and girls need to understand how current and emerging technologies can help them participate in the economy and society. They also need to be aware of their rights, including their right to online privacy so that their use of the internet does not lead to discrimination, harassment, and violence. Research from the wider Asia and Pacific region suggests that women prefer to learn about the internet from friends and families, and therefore peer-driven training is important (Internet Society 2017). Awareness should also be raised on digital platforms, which can allow women entrepreneurs to reach a wider range of customers without incurring expensive marketing and sales expenditures (OECD 2018). Several fintech and digital service providers are enabling women to become entrepreneurs—equipping them with technologies like point-of-sale devices and quick response codes, allowing them to conveniently collect payments from clients (ADB 2020b).

Lower Priority

- **Partner with the private sector to address violence against women workers in the formal sector.** Awareness can be carried out among formal businesses on the costs of violence to business, ensuring that there are company policies on sexual harassment and abuse, support to survivors, and referral to other services, including GBV response services, mental health and psychosocial support, and sexual and reproductive health and rights services. Business for Social Responsibility is currently implementing the HERrespect project, which works across 17 countries and more than 1,000 workplaces to increase gender equality in global supply chains. It is building capacity in companies through critical reflections on gender norms, skills building to prevent and address violence, and joint sessions between workers and management. Management systems are also being strengthened through policies and processes to prevent and address workplace violence, awareness campaigns and monitoring of programs, and linkages to community services and local initiatives.[43]

- **Mobilize capital for women-owned businesses by encouraging financial intermediaries to increase the percentage of loans meeting the 2X Challenge criteria.**[44] The 2X Challenge calls on the G7 and other development finance institutions to collectively mobilize $3 billion to invest in the world's women. While the funding meeting these criteria has been mobilized and has increased significantly in other regions in recent years, it has been more difficult in the Pacific due to perceived or real increased risks. IFC (2018b) finds a financing gap for women-owned MSMEs across many Pacific island countries. The DFAT-funded RISE program has expanded the understanding and interest in gender lens investing in the Pacific and provided a foundation on which to build upon. The focus on private-sector-led recovery from the COVID-19 pandemic in the region may provide an opportunity for development finance institutions to work creatively with financial intermediaries and strengthen their commitments to gender lens investing. Development finance institutions could then publish all 2X Challenge-qualifying investments on their website, as has been done by U.S. International Development Finance Corporation, or in annual reports as has been done by Promotion et Participation pour la Coopération Économique (French Development Finance Institution) (AFD and UN Women 2021).

- **Work with technical and vocational education and training and other educational institutions to increase availability and accessibility of business and entrepreneurship courses for women and increase their capacity to be adequately equipped for work.** There should be courses specifically designed and delivered about entrepreneurship, which are market-driven and targeted around the needs of women entrepreneurs (UN Women 2020). There should be courses both on business start-up and business scale-up. There needs to be an emphasis on learning skills such as creating business plans, conducting market analyses, budgeting and financial literacy, digital/e-commerce, and laws and regulations. As part of these courses, life skills training is also crucial, such as on career management, leadership, interpersonal skills, self-esteem, strategies to balance paid and unpaid responsibilities, and information about reproductive care and family planning. Facilitating linkages with the private sector is also important such as through in-training, mentorship schemes, and internships for women students and those from underrepresented groups. Simultaneous interventions to address occupational segregation, the unequal division of unpaid care work, and the cost and availability of childcare facilities are also important in facilitating women's participation in vocational and business training programs (see Chinen et al. 2017).

---

[43]   BSR. HERproject. HERrespect. https://herproject.org/programs/herrespect.
[44]   2X Challenge. Financing for Women. https://www.2xchallenge.org/criteria.

APPENDIX 1
Research Questions

Woman on mobile phone.

Key Research Questions	Detailed Research Questions
What are the status and trends of women's economic empowerment in the Pacific?	(i) How has women's access to assets, services, and opportunities, as well as voice and agency, changed? (ii) What has changed in the enabling environment for women's economic empowerment, including policies and norms, that mediate women's access to and control over economic assets? (iii) What are the current key barriers to women's economic empowerment in the Pacific, and how do these barriers differ from the formal to the informal economy? (iv) How is climate change affecting the status and trends of women's economic empowerment in the Pacific? (v) How is access to digital technologies affecting the status and trends of women's economic empowerment in the Pacific? (vi) What progress have development partners and governments made toward increasing women's access to employment and control over income, and what are the current gaps?
How are women owning, formalizing, and expanding their businesses?	(i) Why do women work in the informal economy, and where in the informal economy hierarchy are women positioned? (ii) What are the status and trends of women's entrepreneurship and women-owned MSMEs (e.g., size of business, ownership structures)? (iii) How are women-owned MSMEs in the formal economy expanding? (iv) What are the key barriers for women entrepreneurs and women-owned MSMEs in the expansion and formalization of their businesses? (v) What are the risks or potential risks for women in the formalization of their MSME? To what extent have these risks been mitigated? (vi) Who is providing capital for and investing into women-owned businesses? How has this changed? (vii) What is the status of social impact investing/gender lens investing? (viii) How does access to finance, digital technology, and other resources help women in business, including in business expansion? (ix) How has the legal and regulatory environment changed to be more responsive to women-owned MSMEs and women entrepreneurs? What lessons have been learned? (x) To what extent are women entrepreneurs and women-owned MSMEs organizing and networking to shift the enabling environment?
What is the association between women's economic empowerment and violence against women and girls for women entrepreneurs and women-owned MSMEs in the Pacific?	(i) What are the intersections between women's economic empowerment and VAWG in the Pacific, for women-owned MSMEs and women entrepreneurs? (ii) What interventions by governments, development partners, civil society, or the private sector have addressed VAWG for women entrepreneurs and women owners of MSMEs? What evidence is there on the effectiveness of these interventions on preventing and responding to violence?

continued on next page

Table continued

Key Research Questions	Detailed Research Questions
How has the COVID-19 pandemic affected women's economic empowerment in the Pacific?	(i) How have women entrepreneurs and women-owned MSMEs been significantly affected by the COVID-19 pandemic? How has the COVID-19 pandemic altered women's access to resources and opportunities as well as voice and agency? (ii) How effective have government stimulus or support packages been in accounting for the needs of women entrepreneurs and women-owned MSMEs, and in mitigating the impact of the COVID-19 pandemic?
What are the key evidence gaps on women's economic empowerment in the Pacific?	(i) What do we know about what has worked/not worked for women's economic empowerment in development partner programs in the Pacific? (ii) What is the strength of evidence of women's economic empowerment themes/concepts in the Pacific? How does evidence on women's economic empowerment vary across different geographies? (iii) What methodologies are used/not used to assess women's economic empowerment in the Pacific, and how methodologically robust are these studies? (iv) What do we not know about the status and trends of women's entrepreneurship and women-owned MSMEs in the Pacific? (v) To what extent is regional and national data on economic development disaggregated by sex and other intersectional aspects of identity, at the individual level? To what extent is data informing policy on women's economic empowerment, especially for women entrepreneurs and women-owned MSMEs?

COVID-19 = coronavirus disease; MSMEs = micro, small, and medium-sized enterprises; VAWG = violence against women and girls.
Source: Authors.

APPENDIX 2
Strength of the Evidence

Women weaving.

Detailed Research Questions	Strength of the Evidence	Comments on the Evidence	Evidence across Countries
RQ1. What are the status and trends of women's economic empowerment in the Pacific developing member countries?			
How has women's access to assets, services, and opportunities, as well as voice and agency, changed?	Strong	Strong evidence on access to formal and informal employment across countries.	Overall, there is more evidence for Fiji, Papua New Guinea, Solomon Islands, and Samoa. Less evidence was found in countries with smaller populations, particularly Nauru and Niue.
What has changed in the enabling environment for women's economic empowerment, including policies and norms, that mediate women's access to and control over economic assets?	Medium	Studies tend to concentrate on countries with larger populations.	
What are the current key barriers to women's economic empowerment in the Pacific, and how do these barriers differ from the formal to the informal economy?	Strong	Strong evidence on a range of barriers, particularly land rights and time burdens, across a range of countries.	
How is climate change affecting the status and trends in women's economic empowerment in the Pacific?	Limited	There are a small number of studies on the effects of climate change on women, and limited evidence on its effects on their businesses.	
How is access to digital technologies affecting the status and trends of women's economic empowerment in the Pacific?	Medium	A number of studies have been conducted on connectivity, barriers to access, and the gender dimensions of digital technology access across a range of countries.	
What progress have development partners and governments made toward increasing women's access to employment and control over income, and what are the current gaps?	Medium	Strong evidence of initiatives undertaken by development partners and governments, but limited evidence of the effectiveness of these.	

continued on next page

Table continued

Detailed Research Questions	Strength of the Evidence	Comments on the Evidence	Evidence across Countries
RQ2. How are women owning, formalizing, and expanding their businesses?			
Why do women work in the informal economy, and where in the informal economy hierarchy are women positioned?	Strong	Strong evidence of occupational segregation, and concentrations at the lower end of informal work hierarchy. More evidence on unpaid care work responsibilities.	Overall, there is more evidence for Fiji, Papua New Guinea, and Samoa. Less evidence was found in countries that have smaller populations (i.e., Cook Islands, the Federated States of Micronesia, the Marshall Islands, Nauru, Niue, Tonga, and Tuvalu).
What are the status and trends of women's entrepreneurship and women-owned MSMEs (e.g., size of business, ownership structures)?	Medium	Strong evidence of women who tend to own smaller and informal businesses, and recently how more women are setting up their own businesses. Emerging evidence about how women-owned businesses tend to employ more women than male-owned firms. Lack of evidence of sex-disaggregated ownership in the primary sector.	
How are women-owned MSMEs in the formal economy expanding?	Limited	Only a small-scale survey (n=82) in Kiribati, which highlighted women's agency in responding to demand, as well as their attendance to training and networking events.	
What are the key barriers for women entrepreneurs and women-owned MSMEs in the expansion and formalization of their businesses?	Strong	Strong evidence, particularly on social norms and the role of *wantok* ("one talk")/*fa'alavelave* ("an interruption"), which prevents the building up of savings. Strong evidence on access to finance, fewer business skills, lack of information, and weak voice and accountability systems.	
What are the risks or potential risks for women in the formalization of their MSME? To what extent have these risks been mitigated?	No evidence	No evidence. Evidence is dominated by the risks to women of working informally.	
Who is providing capital for and investing into women-owned businesses? How has this changed?	No evidence	The Pacific Readiness for Investment in Social Enterprise has done work in growing the social impact investment market, but it is not clear which businesses are investing, if any.	

continued on next page

Table continued

Detailed Research Questions	Strength of the Evidence	Comments on the Evidence	Evidence across Countries
What is the status of social impact investing and gender lens investing?	Limited	Impact investment market is nascent in the Pacific and therefore there is little evidence of what works or does not work. Weak evidence of crowdfunding and peer-to-peer funding.	
How does access to finance, digital technology, and other resources help women in business, including in business expansion?	Medium	Much of the literature focuses on barriers rather than the opportunities that finance, digital, and other resources provide. Evidence is stronger on the opportunities of access to finance.	
How has the legal and regulatory environment changed to be more responsive to women-owned MSMEs and women entrepreneurs? What lessons have been learned?	Medium	Mostly evidence on how digital processes has had an unintended but positive effect on women.	
To what extent are women entrepreneurs and women-owned MSMEs organizing and networking more to shift the enabling environment?	Medium	Women-owned MSMEs and women entrepreneurs are networking to support each other but they are not addressing unequal power relations and seeking systemic institutional, legal, and societal changes. Women in Business Development Samoa has achieved considerable success.	
RQ3. What is the association between women's economic empowerment and violence against women and girls (VAWG) for women entrepreneurs and women-owned MSMEs in the Pacific?			
What are the intersections between women's economic empowerment and VAWG in the Pacific, for women-owned MSMEs and women entrepreneurs?	Limited	The link between VAWG and women's economic empowerment in the Pacific is not well-documented. There is some evidence available on violence and harassment in the workplace, including for women entrepreneurs, and the cost of this for businesses.	Overall, the evidence is mostly focused on Fiji and Papua New Guinea.
What interventions by governments, development partners, civil society, or the private sector have addressed VAWG for women entrepreneurs and women owners of MSMEs? What evidence is there on the effectiveness of these interventions on preventing and responding to violence?	Limited	Majority of evidence is based on examples or anecdotes. Early indications of the effectiveness of two interventions are available.	

continued on next page

Table continued

Detailed Research Questions	Strength of the Evidence	Comments on the Evidence	Evidence across Countries
RQ4. How has the COVID-19 pandemic affected women's economic empowerment in the Pacific?			
How have women entrepreneurs and women-owned MSMEs been significantly affected by the COVID-19 pandemic? How has the COVID-19 pandemic altered women's access to resources and opportunities as well as voice and agency?	Medium	Moderate number of survey-based studies but not always methodologically robust. For example, the 2020 Pacific Business Monitor by the Pacific Trade Investment has generated valuable data, but it is not particularly methodologically robust as the sample size is small (n=134) and participants are not well-spread across countries (52 from Niue but 0 from the Federated States of Micronesia, the Marshall Islands, and Nauru).	Evidence is spread across countries.
How effective have government stimulus or support packages been in accounting for the needs of women entrepreneurs and women-owned MSMEs, and in mitigating the impact of the COVID-19 pandemic?	No evidence	Details of government stimulus and support packages are available, but no evidence exists on their effectiveness.	None

COVID-19 = coronavirus disease, MSMEs = micro, small, and medium-sized enterprises, n = number, rq = research question.
Source: Authors.

APPENDIX 3
Recommendations

Women selling fruit in the market.

Research, policy, and program recommendations for each of the topics discussed in this literature review are presented in the following table, indicating the strength of evidence in each of these topics. Recommendations are classified according to priority—low, medium, or high.

Topics	Strength of Evidence	Recommendations		
		Further Research	Policy	Programming
Status and trends of women's economic empowerment in the Pacific	Medium	• Women's economic empowerment status and trends for women from groups that have historically been marginalized more than others (High). • Social protection options for workers in the lower segments of the informal economy, including women-owned informal MSMEs (Lower).	• Enact policies on parental leave that can contribute to the transformation of social norms (Medium). • Regulators, such as central banks or banking authorities, to require sex-disaggregated data to be collected, publicly released and reported (High). • Promote and legislate equal renumeration for work of equal value in ways that suit national contexts (Medium). • Repeal legislation that prohibits women from certain types of work (High).	• Work with national statistics agencies and designers of international surveys to improve the quality of existing surveys and include sex-disaggregated questions (High). • Develop the unpaid and paid care provider economy and infrastructure, such as supporting quality and affordable care services (Medium). • Leverage digital access and increase access to mobile phones for women, accompanied with skills building on digital literacy and scale up promising initiatives. (Medium).

continued on next page

Table continued

Topics	Strength of Evidence	Recommendations		
		Further Research	**Policy**	**Programming**
Formalization and expansion of women-owned businesses.	Limited	• Status and trends of women-owned MSMEs and women entrepreneurs in islands where there are smaller populations (High). • Strategies to influence social norms on women's roles in business (Lower). • Incentives for business formalization, and the entry points and mechanisms for expansion of formal businesses (Medium). • Forms of support for women-owned businesses to become more resilient to climate change (High).	• Reform tax, finance, and licensing policies and systems to remove barriers and disincentives for women-owned businesses to formalize (Medium). • Develop national regulatory frameworks for crowdfunding and peer-to-peer lending (Lower). • Introduce childcare policies to help women manage their own business in the informal economy, or those who want to return to, or stay at work after having children (Medium). • Incentivize gender-responsive procurement processes in the public and private sector (Lower).	• Encourage financial institutions to accept non-land assets as collateral and increase uptake of secured transaction frameworks (High). • Building on good practice and experience in the Pacific, work with banks to adjust risk assessment criteria and models in favor of MSMEs and informal businesses and ensure financial products and services are adapted to women clients (Medium). • Improve access to and understanding of regulations and official procedures (Medium). • Support in-country stakeholders to disrupt social norms that act as barriers to women's businesses, and work with men and boys to support women's economic empowerment (Medium). • Fund women's business networks in the region and raise their capacity to engage in more diverse activities (Medium). • Mobilize capital for women-owned businesses by encouraging financial intermediaries to increase the percentage of loans meeting the 2X Challenge criteria (Lower). • Work with technical and vocational education and training institutions and other educational institutions to increase availability and accessibility of business and entrepreneurship courses for women and increase their capacity to become adequately equipped for the world of work (Lower).

continued on next page

Table continued

Topics	Strength of Evidence	Recommendations		
		Further Research	Policy	Programming
Association between women's economic empowerment and violence against women and girls.	Limited	Interconnections between VAWG and women's economic empowerment (Medium).	Ratify ILO Convention No. 190 on violence and harassment in the world of work and adopt and enforce sexual harassment legislation and policies in employment (Medium).	Invest in evidence-based programming that aims to shift harmful social norms that sustain violence against women and girls in the world of work, with a focus on women entrepreneurs and women-owned MSMEs (High). Partner with the private sector to address VAWG for women workers in the formal sector (Lower).
Effects of the COVID-19 pandemic on women's economic empowerment in the Pacific	Medium	Effectiveness of COVID-19 government stimulus or support packages aimed at women-owned businesses and women entrepreneurs (High).		Develop and implement targeted measures to help self-employed women restart their businesses that collapsed or are in "survival mode" because of associated challenges with COVID-19 (High).

COVID-19 = coronavirus disease; ILO = International Labour Organization; MSMEs = micro, small, and medium-sized enterprises; VAWG = violence against women and girls.

Source: Authors.

Glossary

Woman standing outside airport.

Agency	Ability to use endowments (such as education and skills) and take advantage of economic opportunities to achieve desired outcomes.
Asset	Resource with economic value that an individual, corporation or country owns or controls with the expectation that it will provide a future benefit.
Economic abuse/violence	Economic abuse and/or violence involves making or attempting to make a person financially dependent by maintaining total control over financial resources, withholding access to money, and/or forbidding attendance at school or employment (UN Women 2022).
Gender	The social, behavioral, and cultural attributes, expectations, and norms associated with being male or female (World Bank 2011 cited in World Bank 2016).
Gender-based violence	Harmful acts directed at an individual or a group of individuals based on their gender. It is rooted in gender inequality, the abuse of power, and harmful norms (UN Women 2022).
Informal economy	All economic activities by workers on economic units (for example, households, enterprises or firms) that are—in law or practice—not covered by formal arrangements (ILO 2013b). Formal arrangements entail work that provides legal or social protection.
Informal work hierarchy	Women in Informal Employment: Globalizing and Organizing (WIEGO) defines a segmented hierarchy of informal work. Those in the lower level of the hierarchy—typically women—are "survivalists" in vulnerable and precarious positions with very little element of choice in their position in the hierarchy (Hearle et al. 2019).
Micro-sized enterprise	An enterprise that meets two out of three criteria: less than 10 employees, less than $100,000 in total assets, and has annual sales of less than $100,000 (IFC 2022).
Micro, small, and medium-sized enterprises	Enterprises that meet two out of three criteria: less than 300 employees, less than $15 million in total assets, and has annual sales of less than $15 million (IFC 2022).
Small and medium-sized enterprises	Enterprise that meet two out of three criteria: between 10 and 300 employees, between $100,000 and $15 million in total assets, and has annual sales of between $100,000 and $15 million (IFC 2022).

Violence against women and girls	Any act of gender-based violence that results in, or is likely to result in, physical, sexual, or mental harm or suffering to women and girls, including threats of such acts, coercion, or arbitrary deprivation of liberty, whether occurring in public or in private life (UN Women 2022).
Vulnerable employment	Workers who are self-employed, either without employees (own-account workers) or are contributing family workers (World Bank 2021a)
Women's economic empowerment	Women have the ability to succeed and advance economically, and the power to make and act on economic decisions to enhance their well-being and position in society (Calder et al. 2020).
Women-owned business	• ≥ 51% owned by a woman/women; or • ≥ 20% owned by a woman/women; and have ≥ 1 woman as CEO/COO (President/Vice-President); and have ≥ 30% of the board of directors comprised of women, where a board exists; and • For those women entrepreneurs with a loan from a financial institution, the loan size at origination would be between $5,000 to $1 million (We-Fi 2018).

References

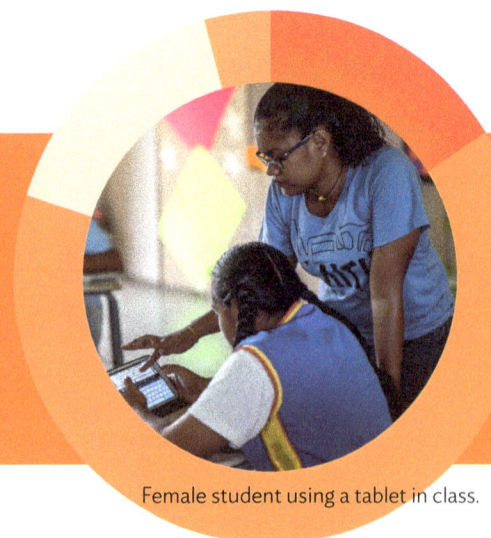

Female student using a tablet in class.

Agence Française de Développement (AFD) and UN Women. 2021. *Public Development Banks Driving Gender Equality: An Overview of Practices and Measurement Frameworks*. Paris; New York.

———. 2020. *Guideline Note on Sex-Disaggregated Data Report Templates*. Kuala Lumpur.

Aldashev, G. et al. 2012. Using the Law to Change the Custom. *Journal of Development Economics*. 97 (2). pp. 182–200.

Alibhai, S. et al. 2018. *Disruptive Finance: Using Psychometrics to Overcome Collateral Constraints in Ethiopia*. Washington, DC: World Bank.

Asia Foundation. 2021. *The Future of Work for Women in the Pacific Islands*. San Francisco.

Asian Development Bank (ADB). 2011. *Gender Issues and Responses in the Pacific Private Sector Development Initiative*. Manila.

———. 2014. *Unlocking Finance for Growth: Secured Transactions Reform in Pacific Island Economies*. Manila.

———. 2015. *Empowering the Other Half: Women and Private Sector Growth in the Pacific*. Manila.

———. 2017. *Strengthening Public Pensions and Health Coverage in the Pacific: Proceedings of the 2016 ADB–FNPF–PPI Forum on Public Pension Systems in Asia, Focus: Pacific Region*. 2–3 November 2016. Manila.

———. 2018. *Women and Business in the Pacific*. Manila.

———. 2019. *Leveraging Trade for Women's Economic Empowerment in the Pacific*. Manila.

———. 2020a. *Governments and ADB's Broader Response to COVID-19 in Pacific Developing Member Countries with Components Targeting Micro, Small and Medium-Sized Enterprises*. Manila.

———. 2020b. Innovative Financial Products and Services for Women in Asia and the Pacific. *ADB Sustainable Development Working Paper Series* No. 67. Manila.

———. 2020c. *Supporting Recovery by Micro, Small, and Medium-Sized Enterprises in the Pacific from the Effects of the COVID-19 Pandemic*. Manila.

———. 2021. *Green Jobs for Women: Construction Skills for Fijian Women*. Manila. 19 August. https://www.adb.org/news/videos/green-jobs-women-construction-skills-fijian-women.

ADB and Asia Foundation. 2018. *Emerging Lessons on Women's Entrepreneurship in Asia and the Pacific: Case Studies from the Asian Development Bank and The Asia Foundation*. Manila; San Francisco.

Asian Infrastructure Investment Bank (AIIB). 2021. *Environmental and Social Framework.* https://www.aiib.org/en/policies-strategies/_download/environment-framework/AIIB-Revised-Environmental-and-Social-Framework-ESF-May-2021-final.pdf.

Australian Agency for International Development (AusAID) Office of Development Effectiveness (ODE). 2008. *Violence Against Women in Melanesia and East Timor: Building on Global and Regional Promising Approaches.* Canberra.

Bafana, B., and N. Hosenally. 2019. Organic Farming Offering Women Entrepreneurs' Access to High-Value Niche Markets. *CTA ITC Update: A Current Awareness Bulletin for ACP Agriculture.* 91. pp. 14–15.

Banthia, A. et al. 2013. *Deepening Financial Inclusion for Women in the Pacific Islands: An Assessment of the Gender Issues Surrounding Women's Ability to Access and Control Financial Resources in Papua New Guinea and Samoa.* New York: Women's World Banking.

Bel isi Papua New Guinea. 2021. https://www.belisipng.org.pg/new-index.

Boniol, M. et al. 2019. *Gender Equity in the Health Workforce: Analysis of 104 Countries.* Geneva: World Health Organization.

Calder, R., S. Rickard, and K. Kalsi. 2020. *Measurement of Women's Economic Empowerment.* Work and Opportunities for Women Helpdesk Guidance No. 2. London.

CARE Australia. 2016. Coffee Industry Support Project. http://www.care.org/work/world-hunger/coffee-industry-support-project.

———. 2020. *CARE Rapid Gender Analysis: COVID-19 Pacific Region.* https://www.care.org.au/wp-content/uploads/2020/03/Pacific-RGA-FINAL-APPROVED-26March2020.pdf.

CARE Australia and UNFPA. 2020. *Linking Women's Economic Empowerment, Eliminating Gender-Based Violence and Enabling Sexual and Reproductive Health and Rights.* https://www.care.org.au/wp-content/uploads/2020/12/201202_UNFPA-CARE_Linking-womens-economic-empowerment-final-1.pdf.

Center for Humanitarian Leadership. 2020. *A Feminist Future for the Pacific: Working Paper 009.* Melbourne.

Center for International Private Enterprise (CIPE). 2020. *COVID-19's Arrival in Papua New Guinea: Impacts on Papua New Guinea Women-Owned and -Operated MSMEs.* Washington, DC.

———. 2021. *COVID-19's Impact on Women-Owned and -Operated MSME's in Papua New Guinea.* Washington, DC.

Center for Women's Global Leadership. 2021. *Interview: Fiji Women's Rights Movement Reflects on Women Workers, ILO C190, and Global 16 Days Campaign.* Global 16 Days Campaign. https://16dayscampaign.org/2020/08/05/interview-fiji-womens-rights-movement-reflects-on-women-workers-ilo-c190-and-global-16-days-campaign/.

Chai, Y. et al. 2022. Does Enhancing Paid Maternity Leave Policy Help Promote Gender Equality? Evidence from 31 Low- and Middle-Income Countries. *Gender Issues.* 39. pp. 335–367.

Chattier, P. 2014. Measuring Poverty as If Gender Matters: Perspectives from Fieldwork in Fiji. *SSGM Discussion Paper* 2014/10. Canberra: Australian National University.

Chen, M. A. 2012. The Informal Economy: Definitions, Theories and Policies. *WIEGO Working Paper* No. 1. Manchester: Women in Informal Employment Globalizing and Organizing.

Chinen, M. et al. 2017. Vocational and Business Training to Improve Women's Labor Market Outcomes in Low- and Middle-Income Countries: A Systematic Review. *Campbell Systematic Reviews*. 16. pp. 1–195.

Chopra, D., and M. Krishnan. 2019. *Linking Family-Friendly Policies to Women's Economic Empowerment: An Evidence Brief*. New York: United Nations Children's Fund.

Cicchiello, A. F. F., and A. Kazemikhasragh. 2022. Tackling Gender Bias in Equity Crowdfunding: An Exploratory Study of Investment Behavior of Latin American Investors. *European Business Review*. 34 (3): 370–395.

Clarke, D., and P. Azzopardi. 2017. *State of Pacific Youth 2017*. Suva: United Nations Population Fund (UNFPA).

Combaz, E. 2018. *Models of Gender-Sensitive Procurement Used by International Aid Entities: K4D Helpdesk Report*. Brighton: Institute of Development Studies.

Congrave, J., A. Shaw, and M. Thomas. 2020. *Women's Economic Empowerment and Standards and Regulatory Reform: A Review of the Key Issues—Evidence of What Works and Measurement Tools. Work and Opportunities for Women Helpdesk Query No. 4*. WOW Helpdesk. London.

COVID-19 Response Gender Working Group. 2020. *Gendered Impacts of COVID on Women in Fiji*. Fiji Women's Rights Movement. Suva.

Curry, G.N., Dumu, E., Koczberski, G. 2016. Bridging the Digital Divide: Everyday Use of Mobile Phones Among Market Sellers in Papua New Guinea. In: Robertson, M. (eds) *Communicating, Networking: Interacting. SpringerBriefs in Global Understanding*. Springer, Cham. https://doi.org/10.1007/978-3-319-45471-9_5.

Curtain, R. et al. 2016. *Pacific Possible: Labor Mobility—The Ten-Billion-Dollar Prize*. Washington, DC: World Bank; Canberra: Australian National University.

Dahal, S., and S. Wagle. 2020. *Rapid Policy Appraisal on Employment, MSMEs and the Informal Sector in Fiji in the Time of COVID-19*. New York: United Nations Development Programme.

Darko, E., D. Walker, and W. Smith. 2015. *Gender Violence in Papua New Guinea: The Cost to Business*. London: Overseas Development Institute.

Defait, V. 2018. Samoa: Responding to Market Demand with Farmer Data. *Spore* (190): 24–25.

Department for International Development (DFID). 2013. *How to Note: Assessing the Strength of Evidence*. https://www.gov.uk/government/publications/how-to-note-assessing-the-strength-of-evidence.

Department of Foreign Affairs and Trade (DFAT). 2019. *Pacific Women Shaping Pacific Development: Cook Islands Country Plan Summary*. Barton, Australia.

DFAT 2020. *Pacific Women Shaping Pacific Development: Six-Year Evaluation Report*. Barton, Australia.

Diverse Voices and Action (DIVA) for Equality. 2019. *Unjust, Unequal, Unstoppable: Fiji Lesbians, Bisexual Women, Transmen and Gender Non-Conforming People Tipping the Scales Toward Justice*. Suva.

Eves, R. et al. 2018. *Do No Harm Research*: Bougainville. Canberra: Department of Pacific Affairs.

Fiji Women's Crisis Center (FWCC). 2013. *Somebody's Life, Everybody's Business! Fiji Women's Crisis Center, 2013. National Research on Women's Health and Life Experiences in Fiji (2010/11): A Survey Exploring the Prevalence, Incidence and Attitudes to Intimate Partner Violence in Fiji*. Suva.

Fiji Women's Rights Movement. 2016. *Sexual harassment in the Workplace in Fiji-2016 Follow-up study*. http://www.fwrm.org.fj/images/fwrm2017/publications/analysis/External-SH-WriteUP-MG-Final-1.pdf.

Finau, G. et al. 2016. Perceptions of Digital Financial Services in Rural Fiji. *Information Technologies and International Development*. 12 (4).

Fleming, F. 2019. *Review of Spa Academy Rural Scholarship Program. Pacific Women Shaping Pacific Development Support Unit.* https://pacificwomen.org/wp-content/uploads/2019/07/Spa-Academy-Review-Report_July-2019.pdf.

Fleming, F., and M. Tabualevu. 2018. *UN Women Markets for Change Midterm Review Report.* Barton: DFAT. https://www.dfat.gov.au/sites/default/files/markets-for-change-independent-mid-term-review-2018.pdf.

Fleming, F. et al. 2020. *Promising Practices in Preventing and Eliminating Violence Against Women and Girls in Fiji.* Suva: Fiji Women's Fund.

Food and Agriculture Organization (FAO). 2019. *Country Assessment of Agriculture and the Rural Sector in Samoa.* Rome.

FAO and Pacific Community (SPC). 2019. *Country Assessment of Agriculture and the Rural Sector in Fiji.* Rome.

Gerawa, M. 2015. The Bride Price Tradition in Papua New Guinea *Women Across Frontiers.* https://wafmag.org/2015/11/bride-price-tradition-papua-new-guinea/.

Global Banking Alliance (GBA). 2019. *Measuring Women's Financial Inclusion: The Value of Sex-Disaggregated Data.* Global Banking Alliance in partnership with Data2X with the Multilateral Investment Fund of the Inter-American Development Bank.

Global Women's Institute. 2014. *Violence Against Women and Girls: Initiate, Innovate, Integrate.* Washington, DC: Inter-American Development Bank and World Bank. https://www.worldbank.org/content/dam/Worldbank/document/Gender/VAWG%20Resource%20Guide%20Introduction%20July%202014.pdf.

Gonzales, C. et al. 2015. *Fair Play: More Equal Laws Boost Female Labor Force Participation. IMF Staff Discussion Note.* SDN/15/02. Washington, DC: International Monetary Fund. February.

Government of Papua New Guinea, National Statistical Office. 2012. *Papua New Guinea Household Income and Expenditure Survey, 2009–2010.* Port Moresby.

Government of Samoa. 2020. *SDG Voluntary National Review.* Apia.

Government of Samoa, Ministry of Women, Community and Social Development. 2018. Empowering Communities to Lead Inclusive Development for Quality of Life for All. *Annual Report 2016–2017.* https://www.palemene.ws/wp-content/uploads/MWCSD-English-FINAL-AR-16-17.pdf.

Government of the Cook Islands. 2012. *Cook Islands 2012 Gender Profile.* Avarua.

GSMA. 2014. *Connected Women: Striving and Surviving in Papua New Guinea: Exploring the Lives of Women at the Base of the Pyramid.* London.

———. 2020. *The Mobile Economy Pacific Islands 2019.* London.

———. 2021. *Connected Women: The Mobile Gender Gap Report 2021.* London.

Hamilton, W. 2020. *Action on COVID19 and Gender: A Policy Review from Fiji.* London: ALIGN.

Hearle, C., S. Baden, and K. Kalsi. 2019. *Promoting Economic Empowerment for Women in the Informal Economy.* Work and Opportunities for Women Helpdesk Guidance No. 1. London: WOW Helpdesk.

Hearle, C. et al. 2020. *Measurement of Women's Economic Empowerment: A Stocktake of Existing Practices in Measuring WEE in DFID/HMG Economic Development Programs*. London: WOW Helpdesk.

Hearle, C., and W. Smith. 2021. *Women's Economic Empowerment and Disability Inclusion in Financial Services*. London: WOW Helpdesk.

Hedditch, S., and C. Manuel. 2010a. *Gender Investment Climate Reform Assessments, Samoa*. Washington, DC: International Finance Corporation (IFC).

Hedditch, S., and C. Manuel. 2010b. *Tonga: Gender and Climate Reform Assessment*. Washington, DC: IFC.

Hilton, T., S.S. Saif, and J. Khan. 2021. *Pacific RISE Final Evaluation*. Pacific RISE. https://www.pacificrise.org/wp-content/uploads/2021/06/Pacific-RISE-Final-Evaluation.pdf.

Holden, P., and A. Pekmezovic. 2019. How Accurate Are the Doing Business Indicators? A Pacific Island Case Study. *Asia and the Pacific Policy Studies*. 7. pp. 247–261.

Howes, S. 2020. Pacific Labor Mobility in the Media Spotlight. *DevPolicy Blog*. 19 June. http://www.devpolicy.org/pacific-labour-mobility-in-the-media-spotlight.

Inter-American Development Bank (IDB). 2010. *Operational Policy on Gender Equality in Development*. https://idbdocs.iadb.org/wsdocs/getdocument.aspx?docnum=35428399.

Intergovernmental Panel on Climate Change. 2021. Climate Change 2021: the Physical Science Basis, IPCC. https://www.ipcc.ch/srocc/download/#pub-spm.

International Finance Corporation (IFC). 2010. *Gender and Investment: Climate Reform Assessment: Pacific Regional Executive Summary*. Washington, DC.

———. 2013. *Closing the Credit Gap for Formal and Informal Micro, Small, and Medium Enterprises*. Washington, DC.

———. 2016. *Research and Literature Review of Challenges to Women Accessing Digital Financial Services*. Washington, DC.

———. 2017. *Tackling Childcare: The Business Case for Employer-Supported Childcare*. Washington, DC.

———. 2018a. *Making Progress: Solomon Island Businesses Advance Gender Equality*. Washington, DC. https://www.ifc.org/wps/wcm/connect/768208a9-49e4-4bf6-a793-b6bbe3e55794/Making+Progress-Solomon+Island+businesses+advance+gender+equality.pdf?MOD=AJPERES&CVID=mp2v3C2.

———. 2018b. *MSME Finance Gap 2018-19 Update (public)*. Washington, DC.

———. 2019a. *Tackling Childcare: The Business Case for Employer-Supported Childcare in Fiji*. Washington, DC.

———. 2019b. *The Business Case for Workplace Response to Sexual and Domestic Violence*. Washington, DC.

———. 2019c. *Waka Mere Commitment to Action: Improving Business Outcomes in Solomon Islands Through Advancing Workplace Gender Equality*. Washington, DC.

———. 2021. *Workplace Responses to Family and Sexual Violence in Papua New Guinea: Measuring the Business Case*. Washington, DC.

———. 2022. IFC's Definitions of Targeted Sectors. https://www.ifc.org/wps/wcm/connect/industry_ext_content/ifc_external_corporate_site/financial+institutions/priorities/ifcs+definitions+of+targeted+sectors.

ILO. 2013a. *Equal Pay: An Introductory Guide*. Geneva.

———. 2013b. *The Informal Economy and Decent Work: A Policy Resource Guide*. Geneva.

———. 2014. *Decent Work and Social Justice in Pacific Small Island Developing States: Challenges, Opportunities and Policy Responses*. Geneva.

———. 2017a. *A Study on the Future of Work in the Pacific*. Suva: ILO Office for Pacific Island Countries.

———. 2017b. *Improving Labor Market Outcomes in the Pacific: Policy Challenges and Priorities*. Suva: ILO Office for Pacific Island Countries.

———. 2021a. *Enough is Enough: Eliminating Violence and Harassment in the World of Work*. An opinion piece ahead of the 14th Triennial Conference of Pacific Women and the 7th Meeting of the Pacific Ministers for Women. Geneva.

———. 2021b. *Pacific Labor Market Review 2020*. Geneva.

———. 2021c. *Rebuilding Better: Fostering Business Resilience Post-COVID-19*. Geneva.

———. 2021d. We Could All Do with a Bit of Hope. What the Informal Economies Recovery Project Means for Tonga. *COVID-19 and the World of Work*. Geneva. https://www.ilo.org/suva/projects/WCMS_777840/lang--en/index.htm.

———. 2022. *Eliminating Violence and Harassment in the World of Work*. Geneva. https://www.ilo.org/global/topics/violence-harassment/lang--en/index.htm.

ILO and Women in Informal Employment: Globalizing and Organizing (WIEGO). 2020. *Extending Childcare Services to Workers in the Informal Economy: Policy Lessons from Country Experiences*. Geneva.

International Women's Development Agency (IWDA). 2018a. *Do No Harm Research Project Report: Women in Formal Employment Survey*. Melbourne.

———. 2018b. *Do No Harm Toolkit*. Melbourne.

Internet Society. 2017. *Issue Paper: Asia-Pacific Bureau, Gender*. https://www.internetsociety.org/wp-content/uploads/2017/08/APAC-Issue-Papers-Gender_0.pdf.

Islam, A., S. Muzi, and M. Amin. 2019. Unequal Laws and the Disempowerment of Women in the Labor Market: Evidence from Firm-Level Data. *The Journal of Development Studies*. 55 (5). pp. 822–844.

ITAD. 2017. *Pacific Women Shaping Pacific Development- 3 Year Evaluation End Report*. https://www.itad.com/wp-content/uploads/2020/02/Pacific-Women-Year-3-Evaluation-Final-Report-140717-1-1.pdf.

Keen, M., and Q. Hanich. 2015. *The Blue Economy: Plenty of Potential*. Canberra: Australian National University.

Kleinert, S., and K. Mochkabadi. 2021. Gender Stereotypes in Equity Crowdfunding: The Effects of Gender Bias on the Interpretation of Quality Signals. *The Journal of Technology Transfer*. 5. pp. 1–22.

Klinger, B., A. I. Khwaja, and J. LaMonte. 2013. Improving Credit Risk Analysis with Psychometrics in Peru. *Inter-American Development Bank Technical Note* No. IDB-TN-587. New York.

KPMG. 2020. *Fiji – Measures in Response to COVID-19*. https://home.kpmg/xx/en/home/insights/2020/04/fiji-government-and-institution-measures-in-response-to-covid.html.

Lambeth, L. et al. 2014. *An Overview of the Involvement of Women in Fisheries Activities in Oceania.* New Caledonia: Pacific Community.

Lawless, S. et al. 2021. Gender Equality Is Diluted in Commitments Made to Small-Scale Fisheries. *World Development.* 140.

Loayza, N. V. 2018. Informality: Why Is It So Widespread and How Can It Be Reduced? *Policy Brief* No. 20. Washington, DC: World Bank.

Market Development Facility. 2020. *Supporting Women's Agency Through Economic Programming.* https://marketdevelopmentfacility.org/wp-content/uploads/2020/11/Women-at-Work-Web.pdf.

Mastercard. 2021. *Mastercard and Partners to Drive Financial Inclusion in Fiji with New Mobile Payment Acceptance Solution for Women Entrepreneurs.* Sydney. 4 August. https://www.mastercard.com/news/ap/en/newsroom/press-releases/en/2021/august/mastercard-and-partners-to-drive-financial-inclusion-in-fiji-with-new-mobile-payment-acceptance-solution-for-women-entrepreneurs/.

McKinnon, K. et al. 2016. Gender Equality and Economic Empowerment in the Solomon Islands and Fiji: A Place-Based Approach. *Gender, Place & Culture.* 23 (10). pp. 1376–1391.

Mcleod, E. et al. 2018. Raising the Voices of Pacific Island Women to Inform Climate Adaptation Policies. *Marine Policy.* 93. pp. 178–185.

Meleisea, L.M. et al. 2015. Political Representation and Women's Empowerment in Samoa. *Volume I: Findings and Recommendations.* National University of Samoa. July.

Michalena, E. et al. 2020. Promoting Sustainable and Inclusive Oceans Management in Pacific Islands Through Women and Science. *Mar Pollut Bull.* 150 (110711).

Mikhailovich, K., and B. Pamphilon. 2016. *Building Gender Equity Through a Family Teams Approach: A Program to Support the Economic Development of Women Smallholder Farmers and Their Families in Papua New Guinea.* Canberra: Australian Centre for International Agricultural Research.

Mishra, V., F. Odhuno, and R. Smyth. 2017. How Do Perceived Obstacles to Operation and Expansion Relate to Subjective Measures of Enterprise Performance? Evidence from a Survey of SMEs in Papua New Guinea. *Papua New Guinea NRI Discussion Paper* 150. Port Moresby: Papua New Guinea National Research Institute.

Mohanty, M. 2011. Informal Social Protection and Social Development in Pacific Island Countries: Role of NGOs and Civil Society. *Asia–Pacific Development Journal.* 18 (2). pp. 25–56.

Nagarajan, V. 2021. *Women and Women's Business Access to Finance Market Research in Papua New Guinea.* Sydney: Macquarie University.

Oakes, R., A. Milan, and J. Campbell. 2016. Kiribati: *Climate Change and Migration: Relationships Between Household Vulnerability, Human Mobility and Climate Change.* Report No. 20. Bonn: United Nations University Institute for Environment and Human Security (UNU-EHS).

Organisation for Economic Co-operation and Development (OECD). 2018. *Bridging the Digital Gender Divide: Include, Upskill and Innovate.* Paris.

———. 2019. *Breaking Down Barriers to Women's Economic Empowerment: Policy Approaches to Unpaid Care Work in Developing Countries.* Paris.

————. 2021. Promoting Gender Equality Through Public Procurement: Challenges and Good Practices. *OECD Public Governance Policy Papers* No. 9. Paris.

————. 2022. *Tax Policy and Gender Equality: A Stocktake of Country Approaches*. Paris.

Pacific Community. 2017. *Women's Economic Empowerment in the Pacific: Regional Overview*. New Caledonia.

————. 2019. *Gender analysis of the fisheries sector in Federated States of Micronesia*. New Caledonia.

Pacific Data Hub. 2021a. *Stat Data Explorer: Time spent on unpaid domestic chores and care work*. https://stats.pacificdata.org/vis?dq=A.SL_DOM_TSPD.........&pd=%2C&frequency=A&lc=en&pg=0&df[ds]=SPC2&df[id]=DF_SDG_05&df[ag]=SPC&df[vs]=3.0&ly[rw]=GEO_PICT%2CSEX%2CAGE%2CURBANIZATION&ly[cl]=TIME_PERIOD&vw=tb.

Pacific Data Hub. 2021b. *Stat Data Explorer: Impact of Partner Violence on Women's Work Who Work for Money*. https://stats.pacificdata.org/vis?fs[0]=Topic%2C0%7CSocial%23SOC%23&pg=0&fc=Topic&df[ds]=ds%3ASPC2&df[id]=DF_VAW&df[ag]=SPC&df[vs]=1.0&pd=2006%2C&dq=A..VAW_TOPIC_014.........&ly[cl]=GEO_PICT%2CTIME_PERIOD&ly[rw]=PERPETRATOR%2COUTCOME.

Pacific Financial Inclusion Programme. 2016. http://www.pfip.org/our-work/work-streams/financial-innovation/.

————. 2020. *PoWER Women's and Girl's Access and Agency Assessment: Solomon Islands*.

Pacific Islands Forum Secretariat. 2020. *Forum Economic Ministers Meeting: Information Paper No. 4: Economic Empowerment of Women*. Suva.

————. 2021. *Forum Economic Officials Meeting: Information Paper No. 4: Economic Empowerment of Women*. https://www.forumsec.org/wp-content/uploads/2021/07/Economic-Empowerment-of-Women_Final.pdf.

Pacific Peoples' Partnership. 2020. *COVID-19 Impacts on the Informal Economy in Wewak, Papua New Guinea*. Victoria.

Pacific Private Sector Development Initiative. 2017. *Improving Papua New Guinea's Competition and Consumer Framework*. Sydney.

————. 2021. *Leadership Matters: Benchmarking Women in Business Leadership in the Pacific*. Sydney.

Pacific RISE. 2021. *Case Study: Pacific RISE as a Case Study of Gender Lens Investing: Influences on the Field*, Canberra: Australian AID.

Pacific Trade Invest (PTI). 2020. *Pacific Business Monitor: Impact on Female-Owned/Led Businesses*. Pacific Islands Forum Secretariat. July. https://www.pacifictradeinvest.com/media/1591/pti-pacific-business-monitor-wave-4-female-focus.pdf.

————. 2021. *Pacific Business Monitor 2021*: Female-Led/Female-Owned Focus. Pacific Islands Forum Secretariat. https://pacifictradeinvest.com/media/1863/pti-pacific-business-monitor-2021-report-female-led-focus.pdf.

Pacific Women Shaping Pacific Development. 2017. *Women's Economic Empowerment: Synthesis Report*.

————. 2018. *Gender-Smart Safety Resources*. https://pacificwomen.org/stories-of-change/gender-smart-safety-resources/.

———.2020. *Thematic Brief: Gender and COVID-19 in the Pacific: Emerging Impacts and Recommendations for Response.*

———.2021a. From Participation to Power: Women's Economic Empowerment. *Pacific Practice Note Series.* Canberra: Australian Aid. https://pacificwomen.org/wp-content/uploads/2021/12/Pacific-Practice-Note-Series-WEE.pdf.

———.2021b. Gender and COVID-19 Economic Recovery Measures in the Pacific. *Thematic Brief.* Canberra: Australian Aid. https://pacificwomen.org/wp-content/uploads/2021/02/PacificWomen_ThematicBrief__COVID-19-economic-recovery_Apr2021.pdf.

———.2021c. *Pacific Women Shaping Pacific Development Final Report, 2012–2021.* Canberra: Australian Aid. https://pacificwomen.org/wp-content/uploads/2021/12/PW-Final_Report-2012-2021.pdf.

Papua New Guinea Business Coalition for Women (Papua New Guinea BCW). 2021. *Recent Resources.* https://www.pngbcfw.org/.

Prosperity Fund. *Applying the Gender and Inclusion Framework for Primary Purpose.* Unpublished.

Rocha, M. 2020. Promoting Gender Equality Through Legislation Through Regulation: The Case of Parental Leave. *Theory and Practice of Legislation.* 9 (1). pp. 35–57.

Safeguarding Resource & Support Hub (RSH). 2021. *Understanding SEAH and GBV.* https://safeguardingsupporthub.org/sites/default/files/2021-06/RSH_BiteSize_Understanding%20SEAH%20and%20GBV_final.pdf.

Samman, E., E. Presier-Marshall, and N. Jones. 2016. *Women's Work: Mothers, Children and the Global Childcare Crisis.* London: Overseas Development Institute.

Sathye, M. et al. 2014. *Industry Challenges and Policy Barriers in Adoption of Mobile Value-Added Services in Remote Islands: The Case of Fiji.* Australasian Conference on Information Systems. Auckland, New Zealand. 8–10 December.

Sathye, S. et al. 2018. Factors Influencing the Intention to Use of Mobile Value-Added Services. *Economic Journal of Information Systems in Developing Countries.* 84. pp. 1–10.

Secretariat of the Pacific Community (SPC). 2009. *Solomon Islands Family Health and Safety Study: A Study on Violence Against Women and Children.* https://asiapacific.unfpa.org/sites/default/files/pub-pdf/Solomon_Islands_family_health_safety_survey_report_2009.pdf.

———.2014. Women in Fisheries. *Information Bulletin.* Issue 25.

Stuart, E., E. Samman, and A. Hunt. 2018. *Informal is the New Normal: Improving the Lives of Workers at Risk of Being Left Behind.* Working Paper 530. London: Overseas Development Institute.

Thomas, A.S. et al. 2021. Why They Must Be Counted: Significant Contributions of Fijian Women Fishers to Food Security and Livelihoods. *Ocean & Coastal Management.* 205 (105571).

Thomas, E. 2017. *Assessing Gender-Based Violence in Niue.* New York: International Center for Advocates Against Discrimination.

Tuara P., and K. Passfield. 2011. *Gender in Oceanic and Coastal Fisheries Science and Management.* Based on case studies in Solomon Islands, Marshall Islands, and Tonga. Noumea: Secretariat of the Pacific Community.

Tuvalu Gender Affairs Department. 2020. *Rapid Assessment of the Socioeconomic Impacts of the Global COVID-19 Pandemic*. Ministry of Health, Social Welfare and Gender Affairs. https://pacificwomen.org/wp-content/uploads/2020/09/Tuvalu-COVID19-Rapid-Assessment-Report_Leaflet.pdf.

United Nations Children's Fund (UNICEF). 2022. *Reopening Childcare and Early Learning Services: Guidelines for East Asia and the Pacific*. New York.

United Nations Conference on Trade and Development (UNCTAD). 2020. *Women Producers of Kiribati and Their Participation in Inter-Island and International Trade*. Geneva.

UNDP and United Nations Office on Drugs and Crime (UNODC). 2020. *Anti-Corruption Toolkit for Women Owned Micro, Small and Medium Businesses in Fiji*. New York; Vienna.

United Nations Economic and Social Commission for Asia and the Pacific (UNESCAP). 2016. *E-Government for Women's Empowerment in Asia and the Pacific*. Bangkok.

——. 2018. 4. Gender equality and women's empowerment priorities in Fiji. https://egov4women.unescapsdd.org/country-overviews/fiji/gender-equality-and-women%E2%80%99s-empowerment-priorities-in-fiji.

——. 2020a. *Micro, Small and Medium-sized Enterprises' Access to Finance in Samoa: COVID-19 Supplementary Report and Recommendations*. Bangkok.

——. 2020b. *Discussion Paper on Barriers and Opportunities for Women-Led Micro, Small, Medium Enterprises in Samoa*. Bangkok. August 2020.

UNESCAP and United Nations Capital Development Fund (UNCDF). 2020. *Micro, Small and Medium-sized Enterprises Access to Finance in Samoa*. New York.

United Nations High-Level Panel on Women's Economic Empowerment (UNHLP). 2016. *Leave No One Behind: A Call to Action for Gender Equality and Women's Economic Empowerment*. New York.

United Nations Population Fund (UNFPA). 2014. *Population Aging in the Pacific Islands: A Situation Analysis*. Suva: UNFPA Pacific Regional Office.

——. 2015. *Vanuatu Sexual and Reproductive Health Rights Needs Assessment*. Suva: National Reproductive Maternal, Newborn, Child and Adolescent Health Committee, UNFPA, UNDP. https://pacific.unfpa.org/sites/default/files/pub-pdf/4.VanuatuSexualandReproductiveHealthRightsNeedsAssessmentReportLRv1.pdf.

——. 2020. *kNOwVAWdata*. 2020 Regional Snapshot. https://asiapacific.unfpa.org/sites/default/files/resource-pdf/knowvawdata_regional_vaw_map_july_29_2020_final.pdf.

UNFPA Pacific. 2020. *Samoa Gender Dynamics Monograph 2020: Gender and Employment, Income, Households and Assets*. https://pacific.unfpa.org/sites/default/files/pub-pdf/samoa_gender_monograph-sgm_final_web_4oct.pdf.

UN Women. 2011. *Making Port Moresby Safer for Women and Girls*. https://www2.unwomen.org/-/media/field%20office%20eseasia/docs/publications/2014/8/making%20port%20moresby%20safer%20for%20women%20and%20girls%202014.ashx?la=en.

——. 2014. Making Markets Safer for Women Vendors in Papua New Guinea. 11 April. https://www.unwomen.org/en/news/stories/2014/4/new-zealand-increases-funding-for-safe-city-programme-in-png.

——. 2015. *Markets for Change Project*. New York.

———. 2016. *Time to Act on Gender, Climate Change and Disaster Risk Reduction: An overview of progress in the Pacific region with evidence from the Republic of the Marshall Islands, Vanuatu and Samoa.* Bangkok

———. 2019. *UN Women Regional Director Rides in their Seats on Meri Seif Buses.* 30 October. https://asiapacific. unwomen.org/en/news-and-events/stories/2019/10/un-women-regional-director-rides-in-their-seats-on-meri-seif-buses.

———. 2020. *A Review of the Implementation of Small and Medium Enterprises (SMEs) Support Legislation and the Capacity Building Needs and Training Services for Women-Owned SMEs and Women Entrepreneurs in Vietnam.* https://vietnam.un.org/sites/default/files/2021-02/UNW_Review_Eng%20Full_18.12.2020_6.pdf.

———. 2021. *UN Women, All-China Women's Federation Jointly Help Businesses Hurt by COVID-19.* 16 September. https://asiapacific.unwomen.org/en/news-and-events/stories/2021/09/jointly-help-businesses-hurt-by-covid-19.

———. 2022. *Frequently Asked Questions: Types of Violence Against Women and Girls.* https://www.unwomen.org/en/what-we-do/ending-violence-against-women/faqs/types-of-violence.

UN Women and ADB. 2022. *Gender-Responsive Procurement in Asia and Pacific: An Opportunity for an Equitable Economic Future.* New York; Manila.

UN Women and ILO. 2021. *Rethinking Gender-Responsive Procurement: Enabling an Ecosystem for Women's Economic Empowerment.* New York; Geneva.

Upadhyaya, S., and J. A. Rosa. 2019. Resilience in Social Innovation: Lessons from Women Market Traders. *Social Science Quarterly.* 100(6): 2115-2133.

Vilisoni, M. T., A. Vilogorac, and S.S. Safi. 2018. Bula Coffee: Women's Access to Economic Opportunities, the Effects on Women's Agency and their Influence on Social Norms in Rural Fijian Communities. In L. Singh-Petersoh and M. Carnegie, eds. *Integrating Gender in Agricultural Development: Learnings from South Pacific Contexts.* Bradford: Emerald Publishing Limited.

Vitukawalu, B. et al. 2020. Addressing Barriers and Constraints to GESI of Women Seafood Sellers in Municipal Markets in Fiji. *Women in Fisheries Information Bulletin.* No. 31SPC.

Vunisea, A., and F. Fleming. 2019. *Impact of Rise Beyond the Reef in Rural Fiji: An Assessment.* Australian AID and Fiji Women's Fund. https://womensfundfiji.org/wp-content/uploads/2021/11/Impact-of-Rise-Beyond-the-Reef-in-Rural-Fiji-An-Assessment.pdf.

Walton, O. 2012. *Helpdesk Research Report: Women's Economic Empowerment in the Pacific.* Brighton: GSDRC.

Women's Empowerment Principles (WEPS). 2020. Gender-Responsive Procurement: *Guidance Note Principle 5.* https://www.weps.org/resource/gender-responsive-procurement

Women's Entrepreneurship Finance Initiative (We-Fi). 2018. *Creating Finance and Markets for All.* https://we-fi.org/wp-content/uploads/2019/01/Joint-World-Bank-Group-We-Fi-Public-Proposal-1.pdf.

World Bank. 2016. *Gender Action Plan 2016-2021, Fall 2016 Consultative Group Meeting.* Washington, DC.

———. 2020a. *Pacific Region Trade Facilitation Challenges for Women Traders and Freight Forwarders: Survey Findings and Recommendations.* Washington, DC.

———. 2020b. *Solomon Islands High Frequency Phone Survey on COVID-19: Results from Round 2.* Washington, DC.

———. 2021a. *Data Bank: Metadata Glossary – Vulnerable Employment.* https://databank.worldbank.org/metadataglossary/world-development-indicators/series/SL.EMP.VULN.ZS.

———. 2021b. *Female Labor Force Participation Rate (% of total* population ages 15–64; modeled ILO estimate). Washington, DC.

———. 2021c. *Trade Facilitation Challenges for Women Traders and Freight Forwarders.* Washington, DC.

———. 2021d. *Women, Business and the Law.* https://wbl.worldbank.org/en/wbl.

World Bank and Cambridge Centre for Alternative Finance (CCAF). 2019. *Regulating Alternative Finance: Results from a Global Regulator Survey.* Washington, DC.

World Bank Group. 2014. The Fruit of Her Labor: Promoting Gender-Equitable Agribusiness in Papua New Guinea. *Policy Note.* Washington, DC. December. https://openknowledge.worldbank.org/bitstream/handle/10986/22405/Policy0note.pdf?sequence=1&isAllowed=y.

World Health Organization (WHO). 2018. *Global and Regional Estimates of Violence Against Women.* Geneva. https://www.who.int/publications/i/item/9789241564625.

www.ingramcontent.com/pod-product-compliance
Lightning Source LLC
Chambersburg PA
CBHW061221270326
41926CB00032B/4798